W9-CXQ-987

FOR REFERENCE

Do Not Take From This Room

WITHDRAWN

Popular
Picks for
Young
Readers

ALA Editions purchases fund advocacy, awareness, and accreditation programs for library professionals worldwide.

Popular Picks for Young Readers

EDITED BY DIANE FOOTE

Association for Library Service to Children

An imprint of the American Library Association
Chicago • 2014

DIANE FOOTE is assistant dean at Dominican University's Graduate School of Library and Information Science in River Forest, Illinois, and is currently serving as fiscal officer and a member of the board of directors for the Association for Library Service to Children (ALSC), a division of ALA. She was a member of the 2010 John Newbery Award Selection Committee and the 2011 and 2012 Coretta Scott King Book Award Juries, and cochaired the ALSC Preconference Planning Committee for the 2013 event that celebrated the seventy-fifth anniversary of the Caldecott Medal. She holds a master's degree in library and information science from the University of Illinois and is a former executive director of ALSC and a former associate editor of *Book Links* magazine. She lives in Chicago with her family.

© 2014 by the American Library Association

Printed in the United States of America
17 16 15 14 13   5 4 3 2 1

Extensive effort has gone into ensuring the reliability of the information in this book; however, the publisher makes no warranty, express or implied, with respect to the material contained herein.

ISBN: 978-0-8389-3605-4 (print); 978-0-8389-3606-1 (PDF); 978-0-8389-3607-8 (ePub); 978-0-8389-3608-5 (Kindle). For more information on digital formats, visit the ALA Store at alastore.ala.org and select eEditions.

Library of Congress Cataloging-in-Publication Data

Popular picks for young readers / edited by Diane Foote, Association for
Library Service to Children.
      pages cm
   Includes bibliographical references and index.
   ISBN 978-0-8389-3605-4 (alk. paper)
 1. Children's literature—21st century—Bibliography. 2. Children—Books
and reading—United States. I. Foote, Diane, editor of compilation. II.
Association for Library Service to Children.
   Z1037.P83 2014
   011.62—dc23   2013044912

Cover design by Kimberly Thornton. Cover image (c) iofoto/Shutterstock, Inc.
Text design in the Interstate and Miller typefaces. Composition by Scribe Inc.

♾ This paper meets the requirements of ANSI/NISO Z39.48-1992 (Permanence of Paper).

Contents

Popular Picks for Young Readers

Appendixes

Acknowledgments

THIS COMPILATION WOULD NOT HAVE BEEN POSSIBLE WITHOUT THE EXPERTISE and hard work of the following Association for Library Service to Children member librarians. I thank each and every one of you for sticking with me through this project with forbearance and good cheer and, most of all, for your knowledge and appreciation for excellent books for kids and your dedication to the young readers we all serve.

Francesca Burgess
Brooklyn Public Library
Brooklyn, NY

Kevin Delecki
Greene County Public Library
Dayton, OH

Caitlin Dixon Jacobson
Schoenbar Middle School
Ketchikan, AK

Loretta Dowell
San Francisco Public Library
(retired)
San Francisco, CA

Teffeny Edmondson
Fulton County Schools
Atlanta, GA

Steven Engelfried
Wilsonville Public Library
Wilsonville, OR

Roxanne Feldman
The Dalton School
New York, NY

Karen Lemmons
Detroit School of Arts
Detroit, MI

Karen MacPherson
Takoma Park Maryland Library
Takoma Park, MD

Claudette McLinn
Center for the Study of
Multicultural Children's
Literature
Inglewood, CA

Mary Milligan
St. Luke's Episcopal School
San Antonio, TX

Ellsworth Rockefeller
Oak Park Public Library
Oak Park, IL

Brandy Sanchez
Daniel Boone Regional Library
Columbia, MO

Tessa Michaelson Schmidt
Wisconsin Department of Public
Instruction
Madison, WI

Laura Scott
Farmington Community Library
Farmington, MI

Eva Volin
Alameda Free Library
Alameda, CA

Beatriz Pascual Wallace
Seattle Public Library
Seattle, WA

Terrence Young
Jefferson Parish Public School
System
New Orleans, LA

Introduction

WE'VE HEARD THE DEBATES BEFORE: "WHY DON'T POPULAR BOOKS WIN AWARDS?" versus "The awards are not for popularity. Popular books have their own awards—they're called bestseller lists!" No books seem to engender such fierce debate as the ones chosen for awards, particularly the Newbery Medal. But the dichotomy between popularity and literary quality represents a false choice that young readers shouldn't be expected to make. There are plenty of high-quality, well-reviewed books that kids love, and here is a compilation of nearly five hundred of them, all recently published.

How did we come up with this vast list? By asking the people who know best: Association for Library Service to Children members from across the country who work with children and books in school and public libraries in rural, suburban, and urban areas. This group represents men and women, those with varying levels of experience in the profession, and those of varying ethnic and cultural backgrounds. They all work, or worked, in direct service to children; since the project's inception, some have retired or moved on to other responsibilities. They were asked to suggest books three times, from among those published in 2010, 2011, and 2012; I culled duplicates and assigned annotations; and the tireless contributors wrote annotations. Here are the criteria we used for inclusion:

- The book must have originated in that format and not be based on a movie or licensed character, such as *Star Wars* or Dora the Explorer.
- The book must be a proven child favorite in contributor's library.
- The book must have received at least two favorable reviews in professional journals.
- Series may be included.
- Contributors were encouraged to consider a wide variety of formats (picture books, graphic novels, poetry, informational books, etc.) and books that reflect all kinds of diversity (ethnic, gender, socioeconomic, ability/disability level, etc.). Recommendations for a diverse collection (DC) are indicated throughout.

As librarians, we know genuine pleasure in books translates into increased time spent reading, which research shows leads naturally to greater reading (and writing) ability and broadens children's general knowledge and awareness. We also know when we make reading recommendations, there's no substitute for familiarity with a child's individual reading ability and interests. No book, even one with starred reviews and awards, is suitable for every reader. But what if you don't know a particular child well? How do you know what kids really like? The books listed here have all been road tested by real kids, in real libraries. Each one is a proven kid favorite, with positive professional reviews to back up the literary quality. Some of them are even award winners!

Happy reading.

—Diane Foote, Editor

Popular Picks for Young Readers

Board Books

Recommendations for cultivating a diverse collection are indicated by "(DC)."

Animal 1 2 3

By Britta Teckentrup. Illus. by the author. Chronicle, 2012. 18p. Ages 0-3

Bright, blocky numbers and stylized animals characterize this introduction to both counting and creatures. Companion board book *Animal Spots and Stripes* (2012) offers a similar treatment for learning patterns.

Clare Beaton's Farmyard Rhymes

By Claire Beaton. Illus. by the author. Barefoot, 2012. 14p. Ages 0-4

This entry-level introduction to rhymes such as "Baa Baa Black Sheep" and other familiar ditties is charmingly illustrated in a folk-art style using fabric, buttons, stitching, and sequins, as are its companions *Clare Beaton's Nursery Rhymes* (2010) and *Clare Beaton's Action Rhymes* (2010).

Hey Diddle Diddle and Other Favorite Nursery Rhymes

By Hannah Wood. Illus. by the author. Tiger Tales, 2012. 20p. Ages 0-3

A collection of favorite folk stories simply and freshly retold are presented here for the youngest listeners. Familiar childhood settings (a child's room, the grocery store) and bright, soft colors make this just right for introducing these tales.

Hippopposites

By Janik Coat. Illus. by the author. Abrams/Appleseed, 2012. 38p. Ages 2-4

It seems like a strange choice to use the shape of a hippo to demonstrate opposites, but it's very effective here. Stylized images of the animal on a clean white background demonstrate "large" (shown next to a mite) and "small" (next to a skyscraper), "squared" and "rounded," "clear" and "blurry," and so on. Sophisticated concepts such as "opaque" and "transparent" may make this a good choice for older and younger siblings or friends to read together.

Potty

By Leslie Patricelli. Illus. by the author. Candlewick, 2010. 28p. Ages 1-3

A diaper-clad gender-neutral toddler tells readers, "I have to go potty!" and decides not to go in his diaper. But where will he go? Young children will enjoy shouting out responses to the toddler's questions: "Should I go in my diaper?," "Should I go in my potty?," "What does kitty do?," and "What does doggy do?" After a bit of squirming, the toddler takes off his diaper and sits on a little plastic potty. Finally, with a "Tinkle, tinkle, toot," he gleefully shouts, "I did it!" With simple text and bold acrylic illustrations, this board book will engage very young readers.

Spot the Animals: A Lift-the-Flap Book of Colors

By American Museum of Natural History. Illus. by Steve Jenkins. Sterling, 2012. 16p. Ages 2-6

Young naturalists learn about colors as well as animals here. Prompts to find the blue animal, or the purple, and so on, are accompanied by die cuts that reveal just enough. Intricate collage artwork is almost photographic in accuracy and detail; additional information is available about each animal for those interested and ready to learn more.

Trains Go

By Steve Light. Illus. by the author. Chronicle, 2012. 16p. Ages 0-3

In this lively board book, seven different types of trains and a caboose speed across elongated pages. Each type of train has its own two-page spread and produces a unique sound, which will entice young listeners to join in. The simple story line will appeal to preschoolers, and the bold watercolor artwork can be easily seen by children seated in small groups.

Tubby

By Leslie Patricelli. Illus. by the author. Candlewick, 2010. 28p. Ages 0-3

Toddlers and adults will both relish the humor here, which is a good thing since little ones will undoubtedly insist on repeated readings. Deceptively simple bold, black-lined illustrations ooze character as they depict a youngster whose bath-time exuberance comically clashes with her parents' good-natured exhaustion. Young readers will adore the way the cheerfully energetic protagonist revels in being naked, creates silly characters from bubbles, and wriggles around the tub. Adults, meanwhile, will particularly enjoy the brief, wry text, which closes with "Mommy dries me. Daddy dries the bathroom." Potty training is similarly addressed in *Potty* (2010).

Picture Books

Recommendations for cultivating a diverse collection are indicated by "(DC)."

1-2-3 Peas

By Keith Baker. Illus. by the author. Simon & Schuster/Beach Lane, 2012. 40p. Ages 4-7

It's the return of the peas from *LMNO Peas* (2010), listed later in this chapter, showing off numbers this time. Beginning with single digits from one to twenty, then in multiples of ten from twenty to one hundred, an appropriate number of the energetic little green peas with their tiny green legs "Rush, rush, rush," "Splash, splash, splash," "Pound, pound, pound," and so on in familiar settings such as a race track, a busy highway, or a firework display. The final double-page spread in this ap-*pea*-ling read-aloud counting book features the number one hundred, with one hundred peas each holding a flag representing its number.

A Is for Musk Ox

By Erin Cabatingan. Illus. by Matthew Myers. Roaring Brook/Neal Porter, 2012. 40p. Ages 6-8

Forget the old saying "A is for Apple." Musk Ox takes over this alphabet book, explaining to his friend Zebra why almost every letter can be used to describe musk oxen. Zebra says, "But musk ox does not start with A." Musk Ox responds, "But must oxen are **a**wesome! Plus we live in the Arctic, which includes some of **A**laska." The animals' comical banter appeals, especially to kids who already know the "real" alphabet. For those who aren't yet sure, images of the musk ox allow just enough of the original item representing each letter to show.

Abe Lincoln's Dream

By Lane Smith. Illus. by the author. Roaring Brook, 2012. 32p. Ages 5-8

Is the Lincoln Room in the White House haunted? The presidential pets who've lived there throughout the years certainly think so, declining to enter the room. In this creative blend of fact and fantasy, a young girl on a school field trip encounters Lincoln's ghost and chats with him, learning about the dream he had the morning he was assassinated and updating him about the current state of the Union and how the country has progressed since his administration. An afterword explains more about what is historical fact in the book.

Acoustic Rooster and His Barnyard Band

By Kwame Alexander. Illus. by Tim Bowers. Sleeping Bear, 2011. 32p. Ages 5-8

Eager to win this year's annual Barnyard Talent Show, Acoustic Rooster forms a jazz band with Duck Ellington, Bee Holliday, and Pepe Ernesto Cruz to compete against such greats as Thelonius Steer, Mules Davis, and Ella Finchgerald. Designed to introduce jazz music to young readers, this lively, humorous story will encourage music appreciation and elicit interesting discussions about the contributions of the great jazz musicians and singers portrayed in the book. Back matter includes a glossary; notes on the musicians, characters, and songs; and a jazz timeline.

All Kinds of Kisses

By Nancy Tafuri. Illus. by the author. Little, Brown, 2012. 32p. Ages 2-4

A sunny fall day on the farm begins with a mama bird kissing her baby and continues with "cheep kisses" for a chick, "mooo kisses for a calf," "maaa kisses for a kid," and so on until "mommy's kiss goodnight." Gentle watercolor and pencil illustrations focus on the kiss but extend the story and possibilities for adult/child conversations with lots of barnyard activity in the background.

All the Water in the World

By George Ella Lyon. Illus. by Katherine Tillotson. Simon & Schuster/Atheneum/
Richard Jackson, 2011. 40p. Ages 4-8

This eye-catching introduction to the water cycle and its importance to life and the earth features a rhythmic text and digital collage-like illustrations. Questions such as "Where does it come from?" get kids thinking, and sophisticated concepts such as evaporation are further explored in kid-friendly terms. Creative type design and textured, ocean-blue art keeps visual interest high and makes science fun.

All the Way to America: The Story of a Big Italian Family and a Little Shovel

By Dan Yaccarino. Illus. by the author. Knopf, 2011. 40p. (DC) Ages 4-8

Yaccarino tells his family history beginning with his great-grandfather Michele Iaccarino in Sorrento, Italy to Dan's family home in New York City. As the subtitle states, a "little shovel" is passed down from generation to generation along with Michele Iaccarino's advice: "Work hard, but remember to enjoy life, and never forget your family." The two-page spreads are alive with color and bold straightforward text. The front endpapers show a simple map from Italy to the United States; the back endpapers show family portraits of each generation in the book. Young readers will identify with strong family values and understand why immigrants sought to begin life anew in the United States.

All Things Bright and Beautiful

By Cecil F. Alexander. Illus. by Ashley Bryan. Simon & Schuster/Atheneum, 2010. 32p. Ages 2-8

Bright, colorful collage compositions vibrantly illustrate Cecil F. Alexander's well-known hymn, which reflects God's creation of animals, flowers, mountains, rivers, sun, and seasons as well as the ability to enjoy all that He made. This song reflects the beauty in the world and the children who live in it; this treatment concludes with a biographical sketch of Alexander and the complete words and music to the hymn.

And Then It's Spring

By Julie Fogliano. Illus. by Erin E. Stead. Roaring Brook/Neal Porter, 2012. 32p. Ages 4-7

This paean to patience focuses on the long wait between seasons, when all is brown and seeds are first planted, until the green begins to emerge.

Here, a boy and his dog sow carrots, sunflowers, and more, portrayed via gentle woodblock and pencil illustrations.

Animal Crackers Fly the Coop

By Kevin O'Malley. Illus. by the author. Walker, 2010. 40p. Ages 5-8

This fractured version of the Grimms' "The Bremen Town Musicians" features a hen accompanied by her animal friends, all of whom aspire to open a comedy club. The humor that characterizes this retelling fits perfectly, therefore, from the animals' jokes being misinterpreted as barks, growls, moos, and the like, to frequent puns that are "udderly" hilarious.

Another Brother

By Matthew Cordell. Illus. by the author. Feiwel & Friends, 2012. 40p. Ages 4-8

In this fresh and funny take on the familiar new-sibling story, Davy, a firstborn sheep, relishes the attention he gets as a singleton, but soon he's joined by twelve additional brothers and things change drastically. In addition to sharing mom and dad's attention, Davy now has a dozen little copysheep following him around. Cartoon-style illustrations capture the silly antics as the thirteen learn to live together, only to face change again when their new baby sister arrives.

April and Esme, Tooth Fairies

By Bob Graham. Illus. by the author. Candlewick, 2010. 40p. Ages 5-7

April takes the call on her cell phone: ". . . You want US? We shall be there. I PROMISE." Although she and her little sister Esme have not done a solo tooth visit before, the young tooth fairies are determined to get their parents' permission to try. "Darlings, you're far too young," says their mother, sporting tattoos and iridescent wings. Their ponytailed father agrees, but the sisters appeal. When finally given the OK, April and Esme take their nocturnal task quite seriously, handling unforeseen situations with pluck. Tender rites of passage are depicted with humor and magic in this tale of two sisters.

Art & Max

By David Wiesner. Illus. by the author. Clarion, 2010. 40p. Ages 5-8

Two lizard friends push the boundaries of creativity when one, named Art, says, "You can paint me," meaning his portrait, and the other, Max, immediately covers Art in paint. Pigment flies as Art shakes it all off; when Max washes him he nearly disappears. Both are inspired to new methods in this paean to imagination and inspiration.

The Artist Who Painted a Blue Horse

By Eric Carle. Illus. by the author. Philomel, 2011. 32p. (DC) Ages 4-7

This seemingly simple array of creatively colored animals can be enjoyed on many levels. The youngest readers and listeners can pore over the colors and creatures; students of art will learn about controversial artist Franz Marc, whose work was banned by the Nazis because he was considered a "degenerate."

Auntie Yang's Great Soybean Picnic

By Ginnie Lo. Illus. by Beth Lo. Lee & Low, 2012. 32p. (DC) Ages 6-9

Inspired by the childhood memories of two Chinese American sisters growing up in the Midwest during the 1950s, this memoir tells the story of Jinyi Lo and her sister's enjoyable family visits to Auntie and Uncle Yang's Chicago home. When Auntie Yang spots a field of soybeans, a staple food in China but not yet one widely available in America, she asks the farmer for some and hosts a soybean picnic, which eventually grows into a large annual gathering for Chinese immigrant families, continuing over the next forty years. Folkloric illustrations created with ceramic glaze on porcelain plates suit the charming narrative.

The Baby That Roared

By Simon Puttock. Illus. by Nadia Shireen. Candlewick/Nosy Crow, 2012. 32p. Ages 3-6

Mr. and Mrs. Deer long to have a baby, and one day a baby appears on their doorstep and soon begins to roar nonstop. The hapless new parents seek help from Uncle Duncan, Auntie Agnes, and Dr. Fox, but—how peculiar!—each friend disappears when they arrive to help. Young children will cleverly realize long before Mr. and Mrs. Deer that this is no baby . . . it's a monster, and he's eating everyone up! It is sheer silliness and good fun for storytimes, outreach visits, or the unexpected group visit to the library.

Backseat A-B-See

By Maria van Lieshout. Illus. by the author. Chronicle, 2012. 40p. Ages 3-6

What does a child see from the back seat of a car? This alphabet book follows a road trip down a two-lane blacktop divided by a broken white center line, as street signs are presented from A to Z. The bold, graphic digital images are faithful to the look of real highway signs, even if some of the signs shown might be a bit imaginative, such as "Q is for Quack" signaling a duck crossing and "Z for ZZzzzzz" indicating a hotel for sleeping. Contemporary kids spend a great deal of time in the car; this will help them pass the time while sneaking in a bit of learning.

A Ball for Daisy

By Chris Raschka. Illus. by the author. Random/Schwartz & Wade, 2011. 32p. Ages 3-5

Daisy the dog loves her toy ball; it is her constant companion. When another dog destroys Daisy's beloved ball while they play together, Daisy is downhearted. But time heals everything, and Daisy's mood changes when she gains something special from the other dog. Sequential illustrations of ink, watercolor, and gouache and creative use of lines and colors help the youngest readers to focus on key elements in this delightful wordless story. CALDECOTT MEDAL

Balloons over Broadway: The True Story of the Puppeteer of Macy's Parade

By Melissa Sweet. Illus. by the author. Houghton Mifflin Harcourt, 2011. 40p. Ages 4-8

Subtle watercolors and bright mixed-media collages combine to illuminate this picture-book biography of puppeteer Tony Sarg. Ingenious Tony's love of marionettes and his enthusiasm for tinkering began when he was young and comes to fruition when he gets a job at Macy's department store designing mechanical puppets for their holiday windows, leading to the opportunity for him to invent his trademark "upside-down puppets" that eventually become the Macy's gigantic helium balloons. SIBERT MEDAL

Bea at Ballet

By Rachel Isadora. Illus. by the author. Penguin/Nancy Paulsen, 2012. 32p. Ages 2-5

Ballet is an extremely popular preschool (and beyond) pursuit. This cheerful introduction covers basic movements and positions, the role of the musicians, daily rituals, clothing, and more as a lively group of toddlers attend their ballet class and are ready to learn.

A Beach Tail

By Karen Lynn Williams. Illus. by Floyd Cooper. Boyds Mills, 2010. 32p. (DC) Ages 3-7

Greg's dad gives him two rules to follow during their time at the beach: don't go in the water and don't leave Sandy, a lion Greg drew in the sand.

At his father's suggestion, Greg gives Sandy a tail, which grows ever longer as Greg boldly explores without actually breaking any rules. When Greg realizes he's gone far enough, Sandy's tail serves as a trail to get back and finds his father ready to play. Repetitive use of the phrase "swish-swoosh" and the well-executed, double-page spreads of pastel illustrations make the reader feel like a participant in Greg's adventure.

Bear Has a Story to Tell

By Philip C. Stead. Illus. by Erin E. Stead. Roaring Brook/Neal Porter, 2012. 32p. Ages 2-5

Bear has a wonderful story to tell. Unfortunately, all of his friends are getting ready for winter and are too busy to listen. Instead of getting angry, Bear joyfully helps each of his friends prepare—building a bed for Frog, gathering seeds for Mouse, and more. Finally, Bear himself must get ready to hibernate as well. When spring finally comes, all of Bear's friends finally gather to hear the story, but there is one small problem—he's forgotten what he wanted to say! This is a gentle introduction for children to the themes of patience, friendship, and helpfulness.

Bear in Love

By Daniel Pinkwater. Illus. by Will Hillenbrand. Candlewick, 2012. 40p. Ages 4-8

One morning, a loveable bear discovers a long orange treat—a carrot, which he's never tasted before—outside his cave. The next day there are two more of the delicious crunchy treats, and on the third morning there are three more. Bear is delightfully intrigued and determined to discover the identity of his secret friend, to whom he gifts a honeycomb. Reminiscent of the Winnie-the-Pooh stories, the gentle storytelling here combines with large, soft illustrations to offer a satisfying friendship tale.

Beautiful Oops!

By Barney Saltzberg. Illus. by the author. Workman, 2010. 32p. Ages 3-8

The small-format interactive book takes readers on a creative journey by demonstrating the beauty in a spill, bent paper, scrap of paper, a smudge and a smear, a stain, and a hole. On two-page spreads with lift-the-flap pages, the mistakes are transformed into surprising revelations of various shapes and images with endless possibilities. Childlike artwork and an appealing subject are combined to inspire creativity and the value of making lemons into lemonade.

Big Red Lollipop

By Rukhsana Kahn. Illus. by Sophie Blackall. Viking, 2010. 40p. (DC) Ages 5-9

Rubina is invited to her friend's birthday party, but her younger sister, Sana, insists on coming along with her. Mom, unaware of what a birthday party is, insists that Rubina bring her little sister along. The appealing soft-colored illustrations are expressive, playful, and detailed. This charming story about a Pakistani family will elicit stimulating discussions about the immigrant experience, differences in birthday traditions, big sister/little sister relations, sibling rivalry, and sibling friendship.

Blackout

By John Rocco. Illus. by the author. Disney/Hyperion, 2011. 40p. Ages 4-7

On a hot summer night in New York City, a neighborhood is bustling with the usual activity. A young girl tries to entice her family members to play a board game with her, but they are too preoccupied with other things that matter to them. Suddenly, the lights in the neighborhood go out and everything changes. Realistic text and detailed illustrations provide a sweet ending to an unpredictable event and might inspire provocative discussions about human behavior. CALDECOTT HONOR BOOK

Blue Chicken

By Deborah Freedman. Illus. by the author. Viking, 2011. 40p. Ages 3-6

A curious chicken awakens from the two-dimensional barnyard images on an illustrator's storyboard. In an attempt to introduce more color to her surroundings, the chicken accidentally spills a pot of vibrant blue paint across the page. The pigment spreads until she and her fellow farm animals are coated in watercolor blue. Luckily, a Mason jar of clear, clean water waits to restore everyone to his or her normal hue.

Blue Sky

By Audrey Wood. Illus. by the author. Scholastic/Blue Sky, 2012. 32p. Ages 2-5

Brief text, cleverly worked into the color-pencil illustrations, introduces sky-related concepts such as "cloud sky," "rain sky," "sun sky," and more. Contemporary families may not always take the time to simply skygaze, but this will inspire young readers and listeners to slow down and look up.

Bone Dog

By Eric Rohmann. Illus. by the author. Roaring Brook, 2011. 32p. Ages 5-7

Friends for a very long time, an old dog named Ella tells a young boy named Gus that he will not be around for long, but "no matter what happens, I will always be with you." After Ella is gone, Gus does not feel like doing anything, but he manages to motivate himself to go trick-or-treating. When a group of unruly kids dressed as skeletons harasses Gus, loyal Ella, now a "bone dog," comes back to help her friend. With a simple text and imaginative illustrations, this warm story conveys the lasting friendship of a young boy his old dog.

Boom Boom Go Away!

By Laura Geringer. Illus. by Bagram Ibatoulline. Simon & Schuster/Atheneum, 2010. 40p. Ages 3-6

A toy gnome wants to play his drum instead of going to bed, just as a kid often might. He is joined by other playmates: an elf, a bear, a knight, and mermaids as they create music on their various instruments. The rhyming text is a cadence of sound and movement, making this perhaps a better choice for daytime than bedtime.

Boot & Shoe

By Marla Frazee. Illus. by the author. Simon & Schuster/Beach Lane, 2012. 40p. Ages 5-9

These doggy siblings look just alike, except one's black markings reach as high as boots on his legs; the other's markings reach as high as shoes. They each like things their own way until a squirrel upends their routine. The rotund pups are endearingly portrayed in muted shades of black, gray, green, and yellow.

Broom, Zoom!

By Caron Lee Cohen. Illus. by Sergio Ruzzier. Simon & Schuster, 2010. 32p. Ages 2-5

It's a beautiful night for flying. Little Witch wants the broom but Little Monster needs it first to clean a mess. Together they get the cleanup done and afterwards Little Witch invites Little Monster to take a spin with her to the sky. This sweetly simple story of few words can be approached from a variety of themes: sharing, cooperation, helping, and a not-scary story for Halloween.

Brother Sun, Sister Moon: Saint Francis of Assisi's Canticle of the Creatures

By Katherine Paterson. Illus. by Pamela Dalton. Chronicle/Handprint, 2011. 32p. Ages 7-10

Beautiful, intricate cut-paper and watercolor illustrations illuminate this gentle read. Alert readers will look closely to find hidden details such as bright ribbons on harvested wheat and sweet woodland creatures sleeping in corners. The text is carefully handled; according to the introduction this is a "reimagining" of Saint Francis of Assisi's classic praise hymn to be accessible to readers from a variety of religious backgrounds and is as much a celebration of seasons and nature as a religious hymn.

A Bus Called Heaven

By Bob Graham. Illus. by the author. Candlewick, 2012. 40p. Ages 4-7

Stella's family is surprised when a bus—destination sign proclaiming "Heaven"—is abandoned right in front of their city home. At Stella's suggestion, her parents and other neighborhood friends move the bus onto the front yard, where it becomes a community gathering spot, complete with a fish, books, checkers, dogs, snacks, and Stella's favorite thing, an old table soccer game. When the bus is towed to the junkyard by the city, Stella uses her game skills to win it back, and the community triumphs. Lively, detailed illustrations complement this story suitable for children from urban areas and elsewhere that may foster discussion about neighbors, friends, and what makes a community.

C. R. Mudgeon

By Leslie Muir. Illus. by Julian Hector. Simon & Schuster/Atheneum, 2012. 32p. Ages 4-8

C. R. Mudgeon, a hedgehog with an inflexible personality, doesn't like surprises. He ends each night in his favorite chair by a fire reading his favorite book, but his routine is disrupted when Paprika, a vibrant, high-energy squirrel, moves in next door. Full of enthusiasm for the world around her, she brings color, spices, and music to the neighborhood. C. R. complains at first, but when Paprika is laid low by a cold and relies on him for help, he realizes he truly has made a new friend and even tries daring new things such as adding salt to his celery soup.

Caveman: A B.C. Story

By Janee Trasler. Illus. by the author. Sterling, 2011. 32p. Ages 4-7

This comical alphabet book is a prehistoric story told in single words beginning with the Acorn that a squirrel and cave man find, only to find themselves chased by a Bear into a Cave where a Dinosaur lies in wait. At book's end, though, they are all friends, snoring Zzzz's in the night. Nevermind the clash of geological eras. Older children will enjoy the nuances of the cartoon-like illustrations and how they elaborate on the sparse text. For sharing with preschoolers, though, try stringing the words together with your own silly narration.

The Cazuela That the Farm Maiden Stirred

By Samantha R. Vamos. Illus. by Rafael Lopez. Charlesbridge, 2011. 32p. (DC) Ages 3-8

¡Viva arroz con leche! In this cumulative tale, a farm maiden whips up a batch of bubbling rice pudding with the help of the farm animals: the cow provides fresh milk, the hen lays the eggs, the donkey plucks the lime, and so on. The simmering pot (cazuela) is almost forgotten as everyone dances in anticipation, but just in time, spoons are at the ready for a feast. Spanish words for the animals and ingredients are introduced and repeated throughout, making this ideal for sharing in bilingual storytimes or classrooms, and at *Día* (Children's Day/Book Day) celebrations. A recipe is included. BELPRÉ HONOR BOOK FOR ILLUSTRATION

Chalk

By Bill Thomson. Illus. by the author. Marshall Cavendish, 2010. 40p. Ages 5-8

One rainy day at the park, three kids discover magic chalk. How do they know it's magic? Because everything they draw comes to life. They draw a sun, and the sun appears. They draw butterflies that flutter away. And then they draw a dinosaur . . . The expressive, photo-realistic illustrations of this wordless picture book capture attention and inspire impromptu storytelling. Take this flight of imagination for class visits, story starters, or just poring over the pictures.

Chavela and the Magic Bubble

By Monica Brown. Illus. by Magaly Morales. Clarion, 2010. 32p. (DC) Ages 5-9

Chavela loves chewing gum (*chicle* in Spanish) and is always blowing bubbles. She spends Saturdays with grandmother going to the market and listening to her stories about growing up in the rainforest of Mexico among the sapodilla trees where her father worked the *chicle* harvest. One Saturday, Chavela buys a new gum, Magic Chicle; when she blows a bubble with this gum it lifts her up and carries her on a magical journey. An author's note about the rainforest and *chicle* harvesting is included, as well as a song with music and lyrics.

Chloe and the Lion

By Mac Barnett. Illus. by Adam Rex. Disney/Hyperion, 2012. 48p. Ages 4-8

Chloe's adventure begins when she encounters a lion while walking through a dark forest. Or is it a dragon? This is the beginning of a disagreement—one that breaks the "fourth wall"—between the book's creators and Chloe for control of the story. Witty bickering is the hallmark of this amusing metafictional tale, a clever presentation about creativity and collaboration.

Chopsticks

By Amy Krouse Rosenthal. Illus. by Scott Magoon. Disney/Hyperion, 2012. 40p. Ages 4-8

As in *Spoon* (2009), Rosenthal and Magoon have teamed up to create a lively picture book about utensils, this time a pair of chopsticks. Chopsticks are inseparable friends, "practically attached at the hip." When one of the Chopsticks suffers a breakage and is "whisked away" by the whisk to be fixed by Glue, the injured Chopstick insists that his friend explore the world on his own while the break heals. "Go! Chop, Chop." Filled with delightful visual and textual puns, this is a humorous story about friendship and independence that will speak to friends of all ages.

The Christmas Coat

By Virginia Driving Hawk Sneve. Illus. by Ellen Beier. Holiday, 2011. 32p. (DC) Ages 4-8

Based on a real experience from the author's childhood, this book recalls an episode at holiday time on the Sioux Rosebud Reservation when boxes of donated clothing arrive. Young Virginia, as the reservation's priest's daughter, knows to let the other children pick first and is heartbroken when a coat just right for her is chosen by another girl. But patience is rewarded when a special box arrives just for the priest's children. Set in a specific time and place and authentic to that history, the emotions here are universal.

City Dog, Country Frog

By Mo Willems. Illus. by Jon J. Muth. Disney/Hyperion, 2010. 64p. Ages 5-8

In the spring, dog is having fun in the country, especially when frog asks dog to be his friend. Throughout the seasons, dog acts like a country frog and frog acts like a city dog. The spare text, clean design, and colorful pencil and watercolor illustrations aptly portray the fun and fellowship the two friends share. But when dog returns in the winter, frog is not there. Young readers experience dog's feelings of heartbreak and loss, and also dog's joy when he befriends a new creature.

Clever Jack Takes the Cake

By Candace Fleming. Illus. by G. Brian Karas. Random/Schwartz & Wade, 2010. 40p. Ages 5-7

What's a boy to do when there's no money for a princess's birthday present? Leave it to Jack to come up with a clever idea! In a fresh take on traditional Jack tales, a boy uses his wits to win the friendship of a princess, overcoming sneaky blackbirds, a toll-demanding troll, and more to make it to the castle on time. Skillful storytelling pairs with endearing illustrations to cook up this tasty treat. Young readers and listeners will share the princess's delight in the pleasure of a tale well told.

The Cloud Spinner

By Michael Catchpool. Illus. by Alison Jay. Knopf, 2012. 32p. Ages 5-8

An environmental message is cleverly couched in this original story with a folkloric feel. A young boy sits on a hill, spinning beautiful thread out of passing clouds, careful never to spin too much. His gift is recognized and abused by the greedy King, who represents a common motif in traditional folklore. Spinning cloth for the King's family eliminates all the clouds, which causes a drought throughout the land, until the ecologically aware princess returns the cloth so the clouds can be restored.

Colorful Dreamer: The Story of Henri Matisse

By Marjorie Blain Parker. Illus. by Holly Berry. Dial, 2012. 32p. Ages 5-8

Henri Matisse (1869–1954) was not expected to be an artist. His parents wanted him to take over the family store, but he got ill just thinking about such a career—as he did when he was sent to study law in Paris and ended up in the hospital. His hospital roommate kept busy painting, and Henri realized that was what he wanted to do. Matisse's youth is portrayed in intricate gray pencil illustrations, but as he discovers his talent for painting, the radiant illustrations of his dreams blossom into colors as bright as the ones in the art he became known for.

Coral Reefs

By Jason Chin. Illus. by the author. Roaring Brook/Neal Porter, 2011. 32p. Ages 5-9

A young library visitor is so absorbed in reading a book about coral reefs, she doesn't notice that corals are magically multiplying in the stacks. When the sea bursts through, along with a slew of aquatic creatures, she gladly explores the wonders of the undersea world. Striking watercolors bring the reef and its inhabitants to life while the girl floats past sea turtles and whale sharks, book in hand. Her fantastic journey is a learning experience too, as the accompanying text conveys a wealth of information about the unique ecosystem in an inventive, appealing fashion.

Creepy Carrots!

By Aaron Reynolds. Illus. by Peter Brown. Simon & Schuster, 2012. 40p. Ages 4-7

Jasper Rabbit just can't resist eating the carrots growing in Crackenhopper Field, pulling, yanking, and ripping them from the ground. But one day, the carrots seem to be following him, and he fears his favorite food is out to get him. Is it his imagination? Do his mom and dad see it happening? Black-and-white illustrations highlighted with bright orange carrots complement this well-paced, not-too-scary story. CALDECOTT HONOR BOOK

Dave the Potter: Artist, Poet, Slave

By Laban Carrick Hill. Illus. by Bryan Collier. Little, Brown, 2010. 40p. (DC) Ages 8-10

Dave the Potter's story is an incredible one: He was an artist and a poet, as well as a slave, at a time when it was illegal for slaves to read or write. Living in South Carolina in the 1800s, Dave crafted works of art in pottery that were not only beautiful but included his own writings inscribed on them. Intricate, compelling collage illustrations contain numerous hidden details that add context to the story of Dave's extraordinary life. CORETTA SCOTT KING ILLUSTRATOR AWARD WINNER

Dear Primo: A Letter to My Cousin

By Duncan Tonatiuh. Illus. by the author. Abrams, 2010. 32p. (DC) Ages 4-8

Charlie lives in an American city and his cousin Carlitos lives on a farm in Mexico. The two cousins write letters describing their lives in their respective countries; their experiences often differ, yet the two share universal truths as well, as they compare family life, their friendships, and more. Includes Spanish text and a glossary.

Diego Rivera: His World and Ours

By Duncan Tonatiuh. Illus. by the author. Abrams, 2011. 40p. (DC) Ages 5-9

Making art relevant by connecting Rivera's sources of inspiration to contemporary everyday happenings, this poses questions such as "Would he paint the way we play?" Digital collages combine elements of ancient Mexican art with current images of kids on cellphones and rollerblades, furthering the affinity between life and art.

Dino-Baseball

By Lisa Wheeler. Illus. by Barry Gott. Carolrhoda, 2011. 32p. Ages 4-8

This inspired combination of two tried-and-true kid favorites, dinosaurs and baseball, will interest fans of both. Of course the premise is ridiculous—dinosaurs playing baseball—but some facts sneak in, such as which of the animals are on the "Meat" team and which are on the "Grass-clippers." Hoops fans will enjoy *Dino-Basketball* (2011).

Dinosaur vs. the Potty

By Bob Shea. Illus. by the author. Disney/Hyperion, 2010. 40p. Ages 2-4

The universal young-childhood experience of learning to use the potty is interpreted here by a young dinosaur's initial reluctance to give it a try. Bold, bright, kid-friendly illustrations take the intimidation out of a process that for some kids is a challenge.

Do You Know Which Ones Will Grow?

By Susan A. Shea. Illus. by Tom Slaughter. Blue Apple, 2011. 38p. Ages 3-5

This interactive introduction to a scientific concept asks kids to predict which will and which will not grow in a series of paired objects. The lesson is cleverly concealed in the guessing game, and brightly colored, somewhat abstract illustrations add to the fun.

Don't Squish the Sasquatch!

By Kent Redeker. Illus. by Bob Staake. Disney/Hyperion, 2012. 40p. Ages 5-7

In this colorful caper, Mr. Sasquatch boards the bus, hoping it won't get crowded because he doesn't like getting squished. At every stop, a delightfully ridiculous hybrid creature (Mr. Octo-Rhino, Miss Goat-Whale) gets on, and despite plenty of room in the bus and the driver's entreaties not to squish the Sasquatch, the passengers manage to do just that. It's all too much for Mr. Sasquatch, who passes out cold, but a barrage of resuscitative kisses saves the day. Draw out your repertoire of funny voices; this demands a lively reading! Great fun for storytimes about transportation, funny stories, and manners.

Don't Want to Go!

By Shirley Hughes. Illus. by the author. Candlewick, 2010. 32p. Ages 3-5

The expressive cover illustration of a pouting preschooler hints at the story to come, which brilliantly transforms the emotional tug of war between Lily and the adults in her life into a high adventure. Forced to spend the day with an unfamiliar grown-up because her mother is ill, Lily discovers the many delights of her neighbor Melanie's house, including a baby named Sam and a rambunctious dog named Bobbo. By the time Lily's dad comes to pick her up, she's got only one thing to say to him: "Don't want to go!"

Dot

By Patricia Intriago. Illus. by the author. Farrar, 2011. 40p. Ages 3-6

This deceptively simple concept book uses a rhyming text and black-and-white illustrations highlighted with occasional pops of color to introduce various ideas. A dot can be light (if the dots look like bubbles), heavy (if it's large and rotund), or yummy (if it has a bite taken out of it). The clean design will appeal to young readers just becoming familiar with abstract concepts.

The Duckling Gets a Cookie!?

By Mo Willems. Illus. by the author. Disney/Hyperion, 2012. 40p. Ages 3-5

The intentional resemblance between the temperamental Pigeon and a toddler or preschooler will be familiar to fans of the series and their tantrum-weary parents. Simple but energetic line drawings further exaggerate the story's inherent comedy, showing how the Pigeon's pique builds toward a massive meltdown because his friend Duckling has a cookie and he doesn't. There's a surprise in store for Pigeon when Duckling actually offers him the cookie, abruptly ending the Pigeon's blustering complaints. But is Duckling really that selfless?

Each Kindness

By Jacqueline Woodson. Illus. by E. B. Lewis. Penguin/Nancy Paulsen, 2012. 32p. (DC) Ages 6-10

The absence of kindness anchors this poignant story about bullying, this time from the point of view of the bully. When a new girl arrives in Chloe's class, Chloe and the other popular girls are cruel about the fact that she is poor, white, and wears ragged clothes. By the time Chloe wishes she could take it back, Maya's family has moved away again. The free verse and realistic illustrations convey a powerful story about the harmful effects of bullying on everyone involved. CORETTA SCOTT KING AUTHOR HONOR BOOK

East Dragon, West Dragon

By Robyn Eversole. Illus. by Scott Campbell. Simon & Schuster/Atheneum, 2012. 40p. (DC) Ages 5-7

This humorous friendship story compares and contrasts common beliefs about dragons in Eastern and Western cultures. East Dragon lives in a lush palace and is highly sought after by the emperor for his excellent advice; while West Dragon resides in a humble cave and must defend himself against meddlesome knights. In respecting and honoring one another's differences, they are able to help the people of their lands do the same.

Edwin Speaks Up

By April Stevens. Illus. by Sophie Blackall. Random, 2011. 40p. Ages 3-7

Mrs. Finnemore is a frenzied and flighty mother of five ferrets. On a trip to the grocery store with her four children and oft-ignored baby Edwin, Mrs. Finnemore's best intentions are no match for the antics of her young. The misbehaving older siblings cause a ruckus while Mrs. Finnemore struggles to recall items on her shopping list. The familiarity of this experience is funny enough, but the real humor lies in baby Edwin's nonsensical babbling. Careful readers will quickly detect that Edwin understands far more than his family assumes.

Eight Days: A Story of Haiti

By Edwidge Danticat. Illus. by Alix Delinois. Scholastic, 2010. 32p. (DC) Ages 5-8

This deceptively simple, emotional story of Junior, a seven-year-old boy trapped beneath his house with a friend after the Port-au-Prince earthquake is heartbreaking in its childlike telling about the experience. Using his imagination and his will to survive, Junior recounts each of the eight days he spent beneath the rubble; his loss is palpable on the day his friend "falls asleep." The color-washed illustrations convey the dichotomy of the beautiful tropical setting and the tragedy of the events.

Eight Days Gone

By Linda McReynolds. Illus. by Ryan O'Rourke. Charlesbridge, 2012. 44p. Ages 3-6

Brief rhyming verses and detailed oil paintings present the Apollo 11 mission to the moon in 1969. The black, gray, and white palette evokes the space setting and the design feel of the time period; vocabulary is kept simple, suitable for the youngest rocket scientists.

Electric Ben: The Amazing Life and Times of Benjamin Franklin

By Robert Byrd. Illus. by the author. Dial, 2012. 40p. Ages 7-10

Biographies of Ben Franklin are numerous, but this one stands out in its scope, attention to detail, meticulous research, and detailed illustrations. Franklin's impressive achievements are addressed topically in rough chronological order, rather than taking a year-by-year approach to chronicling his life. He's a perennial source of fascination and school research project topic, and this resource adds to the wealth of information about him. SIBERT HONOR BOOK

E-mergency!

By Tom Lichtenheld and Ezra Fields-Meyer. Illus. by Tom Lichtenheld. Chronicle, 2011. 40p. Ages 4-8

The alphabet letters live together in one large house. During the morning dash to breakfast, the letter E falls down the stairs and is hurt. E cannot be used until she is fully healed! The letter O is chosen to take her place and so begins madcap chaos. This humorous alphabet book is filled with puns and visual word play such as a newspaper headline that reads "Big Troo Falls on Toony Car!" The cartoon-like illustrations enhance the humor, and the ending features a clever metafictional twist.

Except If

By Jim Averbeck. Illus. by the author. Simon & Schuster/Atheneum, 2011. 40p. Ages 4-6

Surprise! Nothing is quite as it seems until it isn't. Young minds flex and leap with every turn of the page as they find that an egg could hold a baby bird, "except if it becomes a baby snake who will slither along the ground on its belly except if it is a baby lizard." Or the lizard could be a dinosaur, or a fossil that cradles a nest in which there is an egg, which might become . . . Dare we guess? Repeat readings inspire children to describe the events from memory or to create their own imaginative flights of unexpected outcomes.

Extra Yarn

By Mac Barnett. Illus. by Jon Klassen. HarperCollins/Balzer + Bray, 2012. 40p. Ages 4-7

Young Annabelle finds a box of colorful yarn and uses it to knit sweaters that spiff up her world, which begins as a black-and-white kingdom. When it turns out her box of yarn is bottomless, the evil archduke decides he wants it for his own. Spare artwork in ink, gouache, and digital illustrations spiff up this comedic original fairytale. CALDECOTT HONOR BOOK

Family Pack

By Sandra Markle. Illus. by Alan Marks. Charlesbridge, 2011. 32p. Ages 5-8

The story of a young female wolf relocated from Canada to Yellowstone is told with straightforward text and full-page watercolor illustrations. This wolf develops from a young, nervous adolescent into a confident, strong adult who can take care of herself. She meets a mate, has a litter of pups, and the cycle starts again. The engaging paintings could tell the story on their own, making it accessible even to prereaders. Back matter includes a page of resources and facts about wolves.

Farm

By Elisha Cooper. Illus. by the author. Scholastic/Orchard, 2010. 48p. Ages 4-8

Refreshingly free from talking animals and silly situations, this offers a spring-to-fall look at a working farm. Pencil-and-watercolor illustrations, ranging from quiet, two-page spreads of the farm at night to busy spot illustrations of July activities, create visual interest and engage readers. Significant—but well-crafted and appropriate—text explains the reality of farm life without idealizing it or relying on outdated ideas (this farmer uses a computer and cell phone to check crop yields) in this gentle homage to farm life. Perfect for a detail-oriented young reader and for sharing one-on-one.

Faster! Faster!

By Leslie Patricelli. Illus. by the author. Candlewick, 2012. 32p. Ages 3-6

The little girl who starred in *Higher! Higher!* (2009) returns to urge her indefatigable father to new gymnastic feats. This time, Dad is on his knees, with his daughter on his back, and he variously becomes an ostrich, horse, tiger, and so on as her imagination runs wild. By the end of their romp, Dad has been transformed into an exhausted, beached sea turtle, but his daughter remains appreciative, saying, "You're fast, Daddy!" Deceptively simple acrylic artwork is infused with animation and aptly conveys the close connection between father and daughter.

Fiesta Babies

By Carmen Tafolla. Illus. by Amy Cordova. Tricycle, 2010. 24p. (DC) Ages 2-5

Babies know how to have a good time at San Antonio's annual Fiesta celebration! They dip into salsa, sing along to Grandpa's favorite mariachi song, and dance the cha-cha-cha and the choo-choo-choo. Bright illustrations feature playful babies adorned with crowns of flowers and toddling in their own musical parade. With simple rhyming text and sturdy pages, this is fun for sharing with toddlers and young preschoolers. A brief glossary defines familiar Spanish words used in the story, such as *beso* and *mariachi*. BELPRÉ HONOR BOOK FOR ILLUSTRATION

Goal!

By Mina Javaherbin. Illus. by A. G. Ford. Candlewick, 2010. 40p. Ages 5-8

Set in an unnamed South African town, this focuses on six boys, including narrator Ajani. Having won a federation-size soccer ball for his reading skills, Ajani is eager to call his friends to play despite the dangers of bullies. Dramatic oil paintings clearly show how soccer lifts the burdens of everyday life from the youth pictured and allow the details of the environment—decrepit buildings and poverty—to shape the story without overpowering it. When the youth outsmart a group of bike-riding bullies, readers will celebrate with them. Includes a factual endnote.

Goldilocks and the Three Dinosaurs

By Mo Willems. Illus. by the author. HarperCollins/Balzer + Bray, 2012. 40p. Ages 4-7

Kids familiar with the original story will chuckle as soon as they see the title of this super silly reworking. Sly humor captured in deceptively simple illustrations and dry, witty text makes this as palatable to adults who will need to read it again and again as it is to the intended audience.

Good News, Bad News

By Jeff Mack. Illus. by the author. Chronicle, 2012. 32p. Ages 3–7

An optimistic rabbit and a hard-luck mouse share a crazy day. The "good news" of a picnic basket gets cancelled out by "bad news": rain. When an umbrella solves that problem, a gust of wind blows it away. The pair endures further misfortunes including a swarm of bees, a bear in a cave, and a lighting strike, but in the end it's the good news of friendship that prevails. The title words are the only ones used in the book; expressive cartoon illustrations depict each surprising turn of events and portray the characters with warmth and humor.

Goodnight, Goodnight Construction Site

By Sherri Duskey Rinker. Illus. by Tom Lichtenheld. Chronicle, 2011. 32p. Ages 1–6

Rhyming text and oil pastel illustrations portray a variety of construction site trucks as they complete a day's work and retire for the night. Blending a kid-favorite topic—trucks—with a necessary daily ritual makes going to bed easier for those inclined not to want to wind down at the end of a busy play day.

Grandpa Green

By Lane Smith. Illus. by the author. Roaring Brook, 2011. 32p. Ages 5–8

A young boy winds his way through the topiary memories of his great-grandfather's garden. In the beginning, the hedges are sculpted into chickens to symbolize the elderly man's childhood spent on a farm. Later, boxwood bushes are shaped into a cannon when the young boy tells us that his great-grandfather served in "a world war." As the story continues, each life event is celebrated in a towering statue of graceful green leaves. This touching celebration of grandparents also highlights the value of family history. CALDECOTT HONOR BOOK

Green

By Laura Vaccaro Seeger. Illus. by the author. Roaring Brook/Neal Porter, 2012. 40p. Ages 2–5

Who would imagine a whole book could be about just one color? Here, all the nuances of the color green are explored in painterly art with visible brushstrokes and a very brief text that somehow manages to convey a great deal of information. The ecological message is implied rather than explicit, which is refreshing. CALDECOTT HONOR BOOK

Henry Knox: Bookseller, Soldier, Patriot

By Anita Silvey. Illus. by Wendell Minor. Clarion, 2010. 40p. Ages 8-11

This compelling narrative about Revolutionary War patriot Henry Knox begins with Henry's birth and early family life, but the majority of the book focuses on his ingenious efforts as an artillery officer in the Continental Army. Informative storytelling and beautifully textured acrylics bring Henry and his world to life, offering a sense of how Henry's love of books and artillery prepared him for his military service. Additional information on the endpapers and at the end of the book offers more information about this period of the American Revolution.

Henry's Heart: A Boy, His Heart, and a New Best Friend

By Charise Mericle Harper. Illus. by the author. Holt/Christy Ottaviano, 2011. 40p. Ages 5-7

This deceptively simple story of a boy and his dog masks a great deal of information about the human heart, including making heart-healthy food choices, the function and parts of the heart, and more. Bright illustrations keep the focus kid friendly.

A Home for Bird

By Philip C. Stead. Illus. by the author. Roaring Brook/Neal Porter, 2012. 32p. Ages 4-8

A gentle text and loose, child-friendly art come together in this story of an unlikely friendship between Vernon, an active, caring toad, and Bird, an oddly silent new friend with button eyes and painted wooden legs. Alert kids will "read" the illustrations to find out what's really going on, and a twist at the end wraps things up well.

Homer

By Elisha Cooper. Illus. by the author. Greenwillow, 2012. 32p. Ages 3-8

Homer is a peaceful, porch-loving yellow Labrador retriever. As each member of the family prompts him to enjoy the day with them, he politely remains in his sunny spot near the front steps. Rather than picking wildflowers, collecting seashells, or running to the market, Homer finds contentment in simply being part of a family.

The House Baba Built: An Artist's Childhood in China

By Ed Young and Libby Koponen. Illus. by Ed Young. Little, Brown, 2011. 48p. (DC) Ages 8-12

Young's father Baba, an engineer, built a specially designed, extra strong house to shelter them during World War II; this house also featured a rooftop roller rink and a swimming pool! Striking illustrations, including drawings, photographs, and collage, bring Young's memories to life for contemporary readers. Some childhood details will be familiar, such as sharing roller skates with siblings; others will seem more exotic to American kids, such as raising silkworms. A timeline and a diagram of the house layout round out the back matter.

How Did That Get in My Lunchbox? The Story of Food

By Chris Butterworth. Illus. by Lucia Gaggiotti. Candlewick, 2011. 32p. Ages 5-8

Bright, bold, and detailed illustrations that jump off the page take readers on a journey to discover where their food comes from. How did the bread, cheese, tomatoes, apple juice, carrots, chocolate chip cookie, and the clementine get into the lunch box? Follow these foods from fields and farms, to processing centers, and finally to the grocery store. The foods in the lunch box represent the basic food groups in the Department of Agriculture's 2012 food pyramid, available online at choosemyplate.gov. A brief introduction to carbohydrates, protein, dairy, and fruits and vegetables along with healthy tips for eating are included. The thick pages and rounded corners make for quick page turns. An index is also included.

How Many Jelly Beans? A Giant Book of Giant Numbers!

By Andrea Menotti. Illus. by Yancey Labat. Chronicle, 2012. 28p. Ages 5-7

The oversized format here is just right for presenting large and larger numbers, and using something as fun as jelly beans to make the numbers real makes the lesson go down even more easily. These big numbers may seem abstract at first, but they're not so daunting; in fact, you can get to one thousand jelly beans in one year just by eating a few every day!

How to Be Friends with a Dragon

By Valeri Gorbachev. Illus. by the author. Whitman, 2012. 32p. Ages 4-7

When Simon's older sister decides to teach him how to make friends with dragons, she not only includes regular manners like saying "please" and "thank you," but also dragon-specific ones, like not poking a stick into its nose because it might sneeze fire. Young readers will want to befriend this not-too-scary dragon themselves.

How to Clean a Hippopotamus: A Look at Unusual Animal Partnerships

By Steve Jenkins and Robin Page. Illus. by Steve Jenkins. Houghton Mifflin Harcourt, 2010. 32p. Ages 7-10

Throughout the natural world, animals improve their chances of survival by working with other species. A coyote teams up with a badger to catch prairie dogs. Weaver birds share their nests with an African pygmy falcon, who returns the favor by killing their predators. Numerous examples of amazing animal partnerships are revealed in eye-catching cut-paper illustrations. This visually appealing introduction to symbiosis introduces young readers to the habits of many fascinating animals, while also providing an insightful look at the complex fabric of nature.

The Hueys in the New Sweater
(Hueys series)

By Oliver Jeffers. Illus. by the author. Philomel, 2012. 32p. Ages 3-6

The perennial tension between originality and conformity is on kid-friendly display in this first installment in a new series about "Hueys," egg-shaped creatures with stylized arms and legs, dot eyes, and simple mouths, who all look the same, think the same, and do the same things. When Rupert knits a brand new bright orange sweater and wears it, many of the Hueys are horrified. But Gillespie thinks that Rupert being different is "interesting" and dons the exact same sweater as Rupert so that he would be different too. Soon everyone is "different!"

The Human Body
(Lift the Flap and Learn series)

By Pascale Hédelin. Illus. by Robert Barborini. Owlkids, 2011. 38p. Ages 3-6

Each page presents an engaging activity related to one of the human body systems: "lift the flap," "slide the tab," "turn the wheel," or "pull the tab." From birth to growing tall, from pooping to getting sick, and more, here are topics that children are naturally curious about in a straightforward, simple, age-appropriate text. The information is presented in colorful, interactive tidbits and answers kids' most common questions about their bodies. Topics include moving broccoli through the digestive system—all the way through, the five senses, when you are sick, and more. Be warned: while there are many answers here, the intriguing information may lead to even more questions.

I Can Help

By David Hyde Costello. Illus. by the author. Farrar, 2010. 32p. Ages 3-6

Lost in the tall grass, a baby duck is rescued by monkey. A Giraffe, an elephant, and other animals help each other and return the animals they helped to their respective parents. Friendship goes full circle as the baby duck becomes lost again.

I Know a Wee Piggy

By Kim Norman. Illus. by Henry Cole. Dial, 2012. 32p. Ages 3-6

Told in the style of "I Know an Old Lady . . ." this romp through a state fair is not only riotous fun, it's an introduction to colors. The wee piggy with exaggerated large ears and eyes is perfectly happy in brown mud until he wants a little red (tomatoes), white (milk), and so on. The color names are helpfully printed in the appropriate hue.

I Spy Under the Sea

By Edward Gibbs. Illus. by the author. Candlewick/Templar, 2012. 32p. Ages 4-7

There is a great deal going on under the waves here: a counting book, a guessing game, and information about sea creatures. A hint and a bit of an image of a creature are first shown, then the creature itself, from crabs to clownfish to a somewhat scary shark. Kids ready to learn specifics about animals are probably too old to need the countdown from seven, but that makes this a good choice for sibling sharing or buddy reading.

I Want My Hat Back

By Jon Klassen. Illus. by the author. Candlewick, 2011. 40p. Ages 4-7

A bear has lost his hat and asks other animals if they have seen it. They all say no, including a rabbit that happens to be wearing a pointy red hat. After a deer jogs Bear's memory by asking what the hat looks like, Bear dashes back to confront the thief. Later, Bear is asked if he's seen the rabbit, and echoes the rabbit's earlier denials: "I haven't seen a rabbit anywhere. I would not eat a rabbit. Don't ask me any more questions."

While adults and older children will be amused by the devious humor, young children may really wonder where the rabbit has gone.

Ice

By Arthur Geisert. Illus. by the author. Enchanted Lion, 2011. 32p. Ages 4-7

Suffering from exhausting hot weather and lack of water, a group of pigs sail to the land of ice and tow back a large iceberg to cool and refresh their island community. Detailed color illustrations are the perfect vehicle to tell this wordless tale of adventure, mystery, and surprise that may inspire creative thinking and writing, vocabulary development, and storytelling.

If You Give a Dog a Donut

By Laura Numeroff. Illus. by Felicia Bond. HarperCollins/Balzer + Bray, 2011. 32p. Ages 3-7

This installment in the If You . . . collection shows what might happen if an energetic dog is given a donut. Using the same formula as in previous stories, the zany chain of events hooks readers with the familiar—and popular—plot, humorous exploits, and satisfying ending. Bright illustrations on a clean white background complement the clever text.

I'm Bored

By Michael Ian Black. Illus. by Debbie Ridpath Ohi. Simon & Schuster, 2012. 40p. Ages 4-7

This is a perennial kid complaint, addressed here by a young girl telling an equally bored potato (yes, a potato) all the fun things a kid can do, such as spinning around until you get dizzy. Hand this silliness to a kid as soon as they complain of boredom; problem solved!

I'm the Best

By Lucy Cousins. Illus. by the author. Candlewick, 2010. 32p. Ages 3-5

Dog has no doubts about who is the best. Dog is! Dog is the winner in every comparison with Dog's friends. Dog can run faster than Mole, dig holes better than Goose, out swim Donkey, and is much larger in size than Ladybug. Dog's friends sadly acknowledge their inferiority to Dog's winning attributes until they turn the tables on Dog's logic. When weeping Dog reflects that "I'm just a silly show-off" and apologizes to Ladybug, Mole, Goose, and Donkey, the group offers unconditional love in return. This brightly illustrated story humorously relates truths about friendship and knowing oneself.

Interrupting Chicken

By David Ezra Stein. Illus. by the author. Candlewick, 2010. 40p. Ages 4-8

All children and the "little red chicken" enjoy bedtime stories that are read over and over. When it's time for the little red chicken's bedtime story, and a reminder from Papa to try not to interrupt, the fun begins. As Papa reads *Hansel and Gretel, Chicken Little,* and *Little Red Riding Hood,* little red chicken is compelled to interrupt and save the characters from their classic fate: "DON'T GO IN! SHE'S A WITCH!" Papa's and little red chicken's caricatures coupled with full-page mixed-media provide a humorous, warm, and loving complement to the repetitive text. CALDECOTT HONOR BOOK

It Jes' Happened: When Bill Traylor Started to Draw

By Don Tate. Illus. by R. Gregory Christie. Lee & Low, 2012. 32p. (DC) Ages 6-9

This picture-book biography presents the life and times of artist Bill Traylor, a former slave who at the age of 85 began to draw pictures based on his recollections of rural and urban life in Alabama and is now regarded as one of the most important self-taught American folk artists of the twentieth century. Traylor was born on a cotton farm in 1854, experienced the Civil War and its aftermath, and endured joblessness in Montgomery before he died there in 1949. A clear text and remarkable acrylic and gouache illustrations that evoke Traylor's own art bring the man and his work to life for aspiring young artists.

It's a Tiger

By David LaRochelle. Illus. by Jeremy Tankard. Chronicle, 2012. 32p. Ages 3-6

A child narrator leads readers on a surprising journey in this interactive picture book. We spot what looks like a monkey tail in a tree until a page turn reveals "It's a tiger!" An orange and black pillow, a fuzzy snake, and other suspicious objects also turn out to be tigers in disguise. Energetic, thick-lined illustrations are sillier than scary, alternating neatly from hidden picture to tiger and back again, and the refrain of "Run!" is all in fun. The ending offers one last surprise: The tiger turns out to be friendly . . . but what about that hidden crocodile?

Jack and the Beanstalk

By Nina Crews. Illus. by the author. Holt/Christy Ottaviano, 2011. 32p. Ages 6-8

Fascinating photo-collages and a simple narrative retell this traditional tale in a contemporary Brooklyn setting. Jack earns a handful of beans and soon a beanstalk grows taller than his apartment building. Jack climbs the beanstalk and meets a giant, his wife, and a hen who lays golden eggs, as in the familiar version. Jack must work in the kitchen, but once alone he grabs the hen and scrambles down the vine. The giant and his wife follow, tumble to the ground and emerge from the leaves in smaller, normal-human-sized forms; it turns out they had been stuck in the clouds under a spell that was broken by Jack.

Jangles: A Big Fish Story

By David Shannon. Illus. by the author. Scholastic/Blue Sky, 2012. 32p. Ages 6-9

This time, "the one that got away" is Jangles, a very large, very elusive, hard-to-catch trout, who noisily "clinked and clattered" from the many fishhooks and lures hanging from his enormous jaw as he swims in Big Lake. This tall tale recounts various attempts to catch him, culminating in a role reversal: Jangles himself captures a young fishing boy and reels him to the bottom of the lake for some storytelling of his own. Dramatic oil paintings and a colorful text with an unexpected ending aptly convey the exaggerated elements of this exciting fish story that is also a celebration of the bond between father and son.

Jimi: Sounds like a Rainbow

By Gary Golio. Illus. by Javaka Steptoe. Clarion, 2010. 32p. (DC) Ages 9-13

In 1956, Seattle, Washington, young Jimmy heard everyday sounds and was inspired by them to create new ones on his ukulele; this was the beginning of his accomplished artistic and musical career. The picture book format seems to imply this is for kids a little younger than most Hendrix fans, but the sophisticated collage artwork makes it suitable for older readers as well. There is factual information here, but this portrait's real genius lies in how well it translates the feel of Hendrix's music to the printed page. CORETTA SCOTT KING ILLUSTRATOR HONOR BOOK

Jo MacDonald Saw a Pond

By Mary Quattlebaum. Illus. by Laura J. Bryant. Dawn, 2011. 32p. Ages 3-6

This is an ideal preface to nature walks for young naturalists. To the tune of "Old MacDonald Had a Farm," Jo MacDonald visits a pond where she observes, hears, and sketches the various wildlife that populate the area. Reeds swish-swish, fish blurp-blurp, dragonflies whir-whir, E-I-E-I-O. After her visit, Jo shares her sketches with Old MacDonald himself. The afterword describes the various animals that can be found in and at a pond, plus suggested nature activities suitable for young children.

A Kiss Means I Love You

By Kathryn Madeline Allen. Illus. by Eric Futran. Whitman, 2012. 32p. Ages 0-5

Close-up photos of a multicultural cast of boys and girls and a few adults, combined with a rhyming, rhythmic text, demonstrate basic thoughts and feelings for young children just beginning to understand how to express themselves, and understand others' expressions. The cheerful images capture everyday activities such as hugging, sharing, and more. Body language and physical expressions of feelings are linked with their linguistic counterparts, facilitating communication and just having fun.

Kite Day: A Bear and Mole Story
(Bear and Mole series)

By Will Hillenbrand. Illus. by the author. Holiday, 2012. 32p. Ages 3-7

Two good friends from *Spring Is Here* (2011) set out to build and fly a kite on a blustery spring day in this cheerfully illustrated friendship story. The simple text stimulates the senses, spelling out the sounds such as those of the coming storm ("rumble, rumble"). When the kite flies away, the two friends are gratified that it can now decorate a bird's nest.

Knuffle Bunny Free: An Unexpected Diversion

By Mo Willems. Illus. by the author. HarperCollins/Balzer + Bray, 2010. 52p. Ages 3-7

Trixie's beloved Knuffle Bunny goes missing during the transatlantic voyage her family makes to visit her grandparents in Holland. At first Trixie feels anxious without the toy rabbit that has been her constant companion since birth. Eventually her fears are relieved as she thinks of the joy that Knuffle Bunny is bringing to other children. This is the third and final title in Willems's Knuffle Bunny series.

Ladder to the Moon

By Maya Soetoro-Ng. Illus. by Yuyi Morales. Candlewick, 2011. 48p. (DC) Ages 5-8

Curious about her deceased grandmother, a young girl named Suhaila asks her mother what Grandma Annie was like. That night, a golden ladder appears at Suhaila's window and Grandma Annie invites her granddaughter on an adventure to the moon, where they look down at the earth below and welcome people who are facing misfortunes. The bonds of love and the connection between grandmother and grandchild are extended to the people they rescue and heal. Enchanting paintings illuminate the magical text. This inspirational story will stimulate discussions on compassion, love, and humanitarianism.

Laundry Day

By Maurie J. Manning. Illus. by the author. Clarion, 2012. 40p. Ages 5-8

This trip through a busy multicultural, multilingual neighborhood in early twentieth-century New York stars a shoeshine boy who finds a lost piece of red cloth and searches for its rightful owner. Accompanied by a cat, he climbs, jumps, hangs from clotheslines, and helps others along the way during his search. Mixed-media illustrations depict lively street scenes of horses pulling carts; people of all ages in the streets, on their balconies, and on their roofs; and laundry hanging on clothes lines. Back matter includes a "Laundry List of Words to Know" that introduces now-common words that originated in countries other than the United States.

Little Black Crow

By Chris Raschka. Illus. by the author. Simon & Schuster/Atheneum, 2010. 40p. Ages 5-7

The cadence and rhythm of the text makes this especially appealing to young readers and listeners. Boldly colored abstract illustrations complement the action as the little crow makes his journey. Little Black Crow's saga works well as a bedtime story by creating a soothing feel with its repetition and simplicity.

Little Mouse's Big Secret

By Eric Battut. Illus. by the author. Sterling, 2011. 24p. Ages 3-5

Little Mouse finds a delicious apple. It's such a treat, he decides to keep it a secret and bury it in the ground. His animal friends approach and ask what he is hiding. Each time he responds, "It's my secret, and I'll never tell."

Unbeknown to Little Mouse (but not the gleeful preschoolers enjoying the story), an apple tree is growing, growing, growing behind him until, oops, his secret is out. But sometimes secrets (and apples) are better when you share them. This sweet and simple delight of a story captures the childlike thrill of being privy to something special.

Little Pig Joins the Band

By David Hyde Costello. Illus. by the author. Charlesbridge, 2011. 32p. Ages 3-5

Kids will relate to Little Pig, a classic "youngest sibling" character. When the rest of his family find instruments to play from Grandpa's collection, Little Pig is left out because he's too little to play any of them . . . until he finds the perfect fit for himself as the bandleader. Energetic illustrations complement the sparse, funny, and nicely timed text. The lessons about finding one's own niche and the importance of cooperation go down easy here.

The Little Red Pen

By Janet Stevens and Susan Stevens Crummel. Illus. by Janet Stevens. Houghton Mifflin Harcourt, 2011. 56p. Ages 4-7

The Little Red Pen (LRP) has to mark students' papers before they come into class or the world will surely end. The LRP solicits helps from her teaching supply friends who all have excuses not to help her—reminiscent of *The Little Red Hen*. Stressed-out and exhausted LRP rolls into the Pit of No Return (trash can). Using teamwork, ingenuity, and the class hamster, the teaching supply friends rescue LRP. The dialog bubbles, zany conversations, variety of text colors, and full-page illustrations add to the fun.

Little Treasures: Endearments from around the World

By Jacqueline K. Ogburn. Illus. by Chris Raschka. Houghton Mifflin Harcourt, 2012. 32p. Ages 5-8

American parents might call their children "honey," "pumpkin," or "sunshine," but what do parents in other countries call theirs? In Australia, "possum"; in Russia, "dumpling"; in Finland, "hug bunny"; and so on. People all over the world are portrayed in a variety of colors in loose, energetic art in this litany of love terms.

Little White Rabbit

By Kevin Henkes. Illus. by the author. Greenwillow, 2011. 40p. Ages 2-5

As little white rabbit hops along, he wonders what it would be like to resemble grass, rocks, and other examples of nature that he notices. Wordless spreads depict his imaginative musings with gentle humor. A tree-tall rabbit towers above the forest in one example, while another shows a flying rabbit fluttering happily amid the butterflies. The cat he spies is too frightening to wonder about, but it's a quick hop back to the reassuring comfort of home. Thick-lined pencil and acrylic illustrations, rendered in a palette of soft greens with splashes of pink, create a highly appealing visual world.

Llama Llama: Llama Llama Holiday Drama
(Llama Llama series)

By Anna Dewdney. Illus. by the author. Viking, 2010. 40p. Ages 3-7

The holiday season can be full of drama for many adults, and it's especially so for anxious, young Llama Llama. He just can't wait for Christmas to come, and Mama is occupied with so many preparations. Parents and caregivers reading this out loud will inwardly recognize the Christmas Eve meltdown, as well as the happy holiday snuggling.

Llama Llama: Llama Llama Home with Mama
(Llama Llama series)

By Anna Dewdney. Illus. by the author. Viking, 2011. 40p. Ages 3-7

Llama Llama doesn't feel well and needs to stay home with Mama, who unfortunately must give him yucky medicine but also reads him a book before his nap. After lunch, it's Llama Llama, now somewhat recovered, who cares for Mama. Their love is on warm display here, as it is across the entire Llama Llama series.

Llama Llama: Llama Llama Time to Share
(Llama Llama series)

By Anna Dewdney. Illus. by the author. Viking, 2012. 40p. Ages 3-7

Sharing is a perennial challenge for many young children, and here again, Llama Llama shows what it feels like to cope with a challenge. When the "Gnu" girl comes over, at first it's easy to share until she grabs favorite toy Fuzzy. Expressive illustrations convey the animals' emotions, as they do in other books about the anxious llama, *Llama Llama Holiday Drama* (2010) and *Llama Llama Home with Mama* (2011), among others.

LMNO Peas

By Keith Baker. Illus. by the author. Simon & Schuster/Beach Lane, 2010. 40p. Ages 3–6

This oversize picture book offers young readers an inventive and entertaining look at the alphabet. Delightfully personified peas become climbers, investigators, nurses, and even yogis as rhyming text introduces each letter. Brightly colored digital illustrations cleverly showcase the architecture of each letter as peas appear as "judges" with gavel in hand, as "underwater divers" in a sea set between the two sides of "U," as "campers" erecting a tent at the bottom curve of "C," and more. See also *1-2-3 Peas* (2012), listed earlier in this chapter.

A Long Piece of String

By William Wondriska. Illus. by the author. Chronicle, 2010. 48p. Ages 3–5

This wordless—even letterless—alphabet book (a reissue of the 1963 original) is an eye-catching brainteaser. The titular string roams and splays across the pages, looping in bold orange images of an alligator, a bird, a castle . . . all the way to a xylophone, yardstick, and zipper. Younger children revel in correctly identifying the objects on each page, while older children will brainstorm to match object with letter. ("N" will be the trickiest.) Follow up the reading with your own spool of string and fun objects.

Looking at Lincoln

By Maira Kalman. Illus. by the author. Penguin/Nancy Paulsen, 2012. 32p. Ages 5–7

In this inviting introduction to our sixteenth president, brightly colored naïve illustrations aptly complement the child-friendly text describing a young researcher's efforts to learn about Lincoln. Intimate details are revealed that humanize the great man: how Lincoln loved his wife's vanilla cake and the fact that he kept notes inside his tall hat, for example. Creative type treatment distinguishes between wonderings in loose lettering, while known facts are in black typeface.

Lottie Paris Lives Here

By Angela Johnson. Illus. by Scott M. Fischer. Simon & Schuster, 2011. 32p. (DC) Ages 4–7

Introducing Lottie Paris, a creative and ingenious African American girl who lives with her Papa Pete in a house across from the park. In the park, Lottie walks, plays, and slides. At home, she plays "pretend" in her room (which she calls a "castle"), eats cookies instead of vegetables, and gets into mischief. Yet Papa Pete is quietly present and keeps an eye on her. Lively artwork enriches the accessible text. There is never a dull moment in Lottie's world.

The Loud Book

By Deborah Underwood. Illus. by Renata Liwska. Houghton Mifflin Harcourt, 2011. 32p. Ages 3-5

In this sequel to *The Quiet Book* (2010), listed later in the chapter, the simple text is in all LOUD caps and no punctuation. The LOUD sounds explore the many LOUD noises one might hear during the course of a day. LOUD noises can be unexpected, exciting, disturbing, distracting, hilarious, surprising, funny, entertaining, embarrassing, silencing, and soothing. The facial expressions on the stuffed animal bear cubs compliment the LOUD sounds. The warm illustrations are pencil drawing with digital coloring. The bear cub parents express the typical adult gestures when children are LOUD. A great read aLOUD!

Marisol McDonald Doesn't Match / Marisol McDonald no combina

By Monica Brown. Illus. by Sara Palacios. Children's Book Press, 2011. 32p. (DC) Ages 4-8

Explicitly addressing the special nature of being biracial, as opposed to clearly one ethnicity or another, isn't often tackled in children's literature and is especially welcome at a time when more and more families come in a rainbow of colors. Here, Marisol takes pride in not matching: not only her family heritage, but the games she plays (pirates and soccer simultaneously), the food she eats (peanut butter and jelly burritos), and more. BELPRÉ HONOR BOOK FOR ILLUSTRATION

Me, Frida

By Amy Noyesky. Illus. by David Diaz. Abrams, 2010. 32p. (DC) Ages 4-8

Strikingly vivid artwork attracts attention immediately to this biographical snapshot of Frida Kahlo, focusing on her move to join fellow artist Diego Rivera in San Francisco from her home in Mexico. Finding her own voice and expressing herself through art complements the excitement of discovering a new city for Kahlo and will inspire reflective contemplation and conversation among young art aficionados. BELPRÉ HONOR BOOK FOR ILLUSTRATION

Me . . . Jane

By Patrick McDonnell. Illus. by the author. Little, Brown, 2011. 40p. Ages 4-8

Jane goes everywhere with Jubilee, her beloved stuffed chimpanzee. A curious observer of the natural world, she carefully studies the spiders and birds around her. Jane reads about Tarzan and dreams of living in Africa. Gentle watercolor-and-ink illustrations interspersed with rubber-stamped designs capture the young Jane Goodall's dream of living "a life with, and helping all animals." The photograph at the end with her hand outstretched toward a young chimpanzee is an inspiring tribute to this child who grew up to become one of the world's foremost experts on chimpanzees. CALDECOTT HONOR BOOK

Meet the Dogs of Bedlam Farm

By Jon Katz. Illus. by the author. Holt, 2011. 32p. Ages 5-7

Farm dogs Rose, Izzy, Frieda, and Lenore each have distinct personalities and responsibilities; here, each is the focus of a short, sweet story. Rose, Izzy, and Frieda have clear jobs, including herding sheep, serving as a hospital therapy dog, and guarding the farm (all documented with Katz's clear and engaging photos), but Lenore—a black Lab—has a more indistinct role that only becomes clear later, when it turns out she's best at being a beloved companion and friend.

Mini Racer

By Kristy Dempsey. Illus. by Bridget Strevens-Marzo. Bloomsbury, 2011. 32p. Ages 3-6

This rhyming race to the finish line takes young readers on a bumpy ride over bridges, through tunnels, and across rough terrain. You may find yourself cheering for the Dalmatians in the polka dot roadster, the bunnies in the carrot go-kart, or perhaps the snail on his skateboard. With every new challenge along the road to victory, each miniracer demonstrates its unique, and often humorous, talent for getting ahead.

Monkey: A Trickster Tale from India

By Gerald McDermott. Illus. by the author. Harcourt, 2011. 32p. (DC) Ages 5-10

This trickster tale stars Monkey and Crocodile, familiar characters from India's Jataka tales. Clever Monkey wants to cross the river to eat the delicious mangoes while Crocodile wants to catch Monkey to eat his delicious heart. With gentle humor, Monkey matches wits with Crocodile, resulting in some close calls. This playful, simply told story is enhanced by bold textured illustrations of cut and torn paper from India and Southeast Asia that capture the energy of the story and mood of the setting.

Monkey Colors

By Darrin Lunde. Illus. by Patricia J. Wynne. Charlesbridge, 2012. 32p. Ages 4-7

This deceptively simple picture book is not merely a book about colors; it introduces a variety of monkeys who come in different colors. Colors indicate if a monkey is young or old, male or female, and some monkeys have different colors all over. Not all monkeys are Curious George–brown as the recurring phrase "Monkeys come in different colors" emphasizes. Children enjoy studying the bold, colorful illustrations and will enthusiastically point out their favorite monkeys at book's end. Supplemental matter includes brief descriptive facts about the featured monkeys and a world map indicating their homes.

Monsieur Marceau: Actor without Words

By Leda Schubert. Illus. by Gerard DuBois. Roaring Brook/Neal Porter, 2012. 40p. Ages 4-8

Informative yet brief text covers Marceau's life before, during, and after World War II (including details of his heroic wartime activities leading Jewish children to safety in Switzerland), while celebratory—though appropriately somber—illustrations add depth and beauty to the story of this amazing man's life and art. Expertly laid out pages feature close ups, full body shots, and all types of expressive movement. While Marceau may not be the first celebrity kids think to research, this is an exceptional portrait of a heroic and artistic man, with the added bonus of presenting miming as an art form. An afterward, suggested further reading, and source notes complete the package.

Moonlight

By Helen V. Griffith. Illus. by Laura Dronzek. Greenwillow, 2012. 32p. Ages 0-5

Rabbit falls asleep just as the cloudy sky clears, revealing a round yellow moon. The rich, buttery light falls on restful animals and the surrounding mountains, trees, and streams. Dark blue illustrations are illuminated in the soft, golden moonlight, making this a soothing story perfect for bedtime.

More Bears!

By Kenn Nesbitt. Illus. by Troy Cummings. Sourcebooks Jabberwocky, 2010. 32p. Ages 3-6

Who doesn't love a good book about bears? Well, the author wasn't planning to write a book about bears but the readers keep clamoring for "More bears!" So the author adds a bear here, a bear there, bears everywhere, but each time the cry goes up: "More bears!" Soon there are more bears than can fit on the page. What's a harried author to do? Rewrite! A rousing choice for school visits, outreach events, and family storytimes.

My Brother Charlie

By Holly Robinson Peete and Ryan Elizabeth Peete. Illus. by Shane W. Evans. Scholastic, 2010. 40p. (DC) Ages 5-8

Holly Robinson Peete, actress, author, and national autism spokesperson, paired with her daughter Ryan to coauthor this picture book based on their personal experiences with autism. In the story, Callie talks about her twin brother Charlie who has autism, explaining what autism is, the way her family cares for him, and the challenges they face. An author's note offers more facts about autism. This is a kid-friendly, excellent choice for introducing the subject of autism to young children.

My Garden

By Kevin Henkes. Illus. by the author. Greenwillow, 2010. 40p. Ages 4-7

A little girl dutifully helps with her mother's garden. Yet in the garden she imagines for herself, there is no need to weed and flowers rebloom as soon as they are picked; tomatoes grow as big as beach balls, and jelly beans sprout jelly bean bushes. Whimsical illustrations in rich pastel hues bring to life a young green thumb's garden fantasy—complete with chocolate bunnies and invisible carrots.

My Mom Has X-Ray Vision

By Angela McAllister. Illus. by Alex T. Smith. ME Media/Tiger Tales, 2011. 32p. Ages 5-7

Humorous cartoon-style art shows what's really happening in this account from the point of view of an overly imaginative boy. He fights a sea monster (imaginary octopus) in his bathtub and can't figure out how his mom knows what he's up to (she sees water dripping from the ceiling below). It turns out this heroic mom really is one, rescuing an elderly neighbor from a fall in the garden.

A Nation's Hope

By Matt de la Pena. Illus. by Kadir Nelson. Dial, 2011. 36p. (DC) Ages 7-11

Captivating art and dramatic storytelling bring this account of the historic 1938 boxing match between Max Schmeling and Joe Louis to life for contemporary kids. As tensions escalated with Nazi German, the match pitted Schmeling, a German, against the American Joe Louis and united Americans of all ethnicities in rooting for an African American hopeful champion.

The Neighborhood Sing-Along

By Nina Crews. Illus. by the author. Greenwillow, 2011. 64p. (DC) Ages 3-6

Colorful photographs of children in parks, neighborhoods, and the community serve as an ideal background for these familiar children's songs, including "If You're Happy and You Know It," "The Wheels on the Bus," "Row, Row, Row Your Boat," and more. Reminiscent of neighborhood scenes on *Sesame Street*, this brings a fresh face to old favorites.

Night Knight

By Owen Davey. Illus. by the author. Candlewick, 2012. 32p. Ages 3-5

Here's a way to make going to bed a little more palatable: Pretend you're doing something else! The stairs are a mountain to climb, the bathtub is the sea, and a bedroom is a castle with a tower (the bed). Flat, stylized artwork features predominantly gold, orange, and yellow, in keeping with the royal theme of the game.

Nighttime Ninja

By Barbara DaCosta. Illus. by Ed Young. Little, Brown, 2012. 32p. Ages 4-7

While everyone is sleeping, a boy dressed as a ninja tiptoes through the house at midnight. The shadowy silhouette figure is in search of something, but what? Textured mixed-media collages evoke Japanese-style artwork and aptly capture the nighttime setting. The spare text maintains tension as the ninja searches for his goal (a nighttime ice-cream snack), only to be caught red-handed by his mother, who sends him right back to bed.

No Sleep for the Sheep!

By Karen Beaumont. Illus. by Jackie Urbanovic. Houghton Mifflin Harcourt, 2011. 32p. Ages 3-7

Bleary-eyed Sheep just wants a good night's sleep but is regularly interrupted by the other animals who loudly quack, oink, and moo at the barn door. Sheep admonishes each with "Shhh, not a peep, go to sleep!" At rooster's crow next morning, everyone is bright-eyed and rested . . . except for Sheep who snores through the wake-up call. A soporific rhythm gently rolls through lines such as "Then there came a loud OINK at the door, at the door, and the sheep couldn't sleep any more." Kids won't fall asleep, though; they'll happily call out the animal sounds and commiserate with Sheep's predicament.

Of Thee I Sing: A Letter to My Daughters

By Barack Obama. Illus. by Loren Long. Knopf, 2010. 40p. (DC) Ages 5-10

Even if it weren't so well done, this would have enormous appeal due to the celebrity of the first author. Fortunately, the creative presentation, clear text, and large, appealing design show that popularity and quality can intersect. The surface story of a love letter to his daughters overlies introductions to numerous historical Americans, from Georgia O'Keeffe to George Washington, Cesar Chavez to Jackie Robinson, and many more. The story aptly blends a celebration of America with an appreciation for fatherly love.

Oh, Daddy!

By Bob Shea. Illus. by the author. HarperCollins/Balzer + Bray, 2010. 40p. Ages 2-5

Silly Daddy! He doesn't know how to dress himself, get in the car, or water the flowers. His little hippo son has to show him how to do everything! Clever preschoolers love pointing out what Daddy's doing wrong and crying out, "Oh, Daddy!" Make the most of this eye-winking goofiness for storytimes about Father's Day, families, and funny stories.

Oh, No!

By Candace Fleming. Illus. by Eric Rohmann. Random/Schwartz & Wade, 2012. 40p. Ages 5-9

Cumulative, repetitive tales have traditionally been popular literacy boosters, and this is no exception. Chased by a tiger, a mouse falls into a hole, and a series of animals attempt to help only to fall in themselves. It's only when someone bigger than the tiger comes along that the tables are turned. Block-print artwork with thick black outlines lends a folk-loric feel to this original story.

One Cool Friend

By Toni Buzzeo. Illus. by David Small. Dial, 2012. 32p. Ages 4-8

After a visit to the aquarium with his distracted father, the very proper Elliot comes home with a live penguin. His father seems oblivious to the fact that Elliot has a penguin living in their freezer, among other strange happenings. But is he really unaware of what's going on? Whimsical illustrations with a retro look feature black, white, and icy blue tones, and delightfully foreshadow the surprise ending. This story about a boy and his pet is also a touching tribute to the relationship between the boy and his father. CALDECOTT HONOR BOOK

Otis and the Tornado

By Loren Long. Illus. by the author. Philomel, 2011. 40p. Ages 5-9

Heavy rains and strong winds approach the farm where Otis, a little red tractor, lives with his animal friends. When they realize a tornado is com-ing. Otis leads them to hunker down in a muddy creek bed, but someone is missing: the farm's bad-tempered and fierce bull. Mostly monochromatic illustrations in dark gray create drama, especially as the tornado touches down. However, bright splashes of color, such as the red of Otis's paint job, focus young readers' attention to the friendly, helpful tractor.

Otto the Book Bear

By Katie Cleminson. Illus. by the author. Disney/Hyperion, 2012. 32p. Ages 4-6

In this charmingly illustrated tribute to books, reading, and the library itself, Otto "lives" between the pages of a book and loves nothing more than to entertain the children in the house when they "read" him. When they're not looking at his book, he can leave it and go exploring. But one time, he can't get back in; the family has moved away, leaving him behind. He must make his way in the big city alone, only finding his way "home" once he locates the public library.

Pecan Pie Baby

By Jacqueline Woodson. Illus. by Sophie Blackall. Putnam, 2010. 32p. (DC) Ages 3-6

A new baby is coming and Gia is not happy about this. Everywhere Gia goes, everyone wants to talk about the "ding-dang" baby. Gia's biggest worry is that the special bond that she and Mama have will vanish once the baby is born. When Gia finds out that she is not the only one who feels that their bond was special, she learns to accept the arrival of the baby who loves pecan pie just as much as she and Mama. Warm colorful illustrations characterize this story that conveys the love between mother and daughter as well as the positive anticipation of the baby's arrival by her multiracial family, friends, and school community.

Perfect Square

By Michael Hall. Illus. by the author. Greenwillow, 2011. 40p. Ages 5-8

Each day, from Monday through Sunday, a perfect square that begins the week perfectly happily is transformed into something new by being split up into pieces that are rearranged and manipulated. Reassembled, it becomes a fountain, a garden, a park, a bridge, and more. On Sunday, it appropriately gets a rest by turning into a window to look out at everything else. Bold, graphic color illustrations encourage creativity and critical thinking skills.

Pete the Cat: I Love My White Shoes
(Pete the Cat series)

By Eric Litwin. Illus. by James Dean. HarperCollins, 2010. 32p. Ages 4-8

Pete the Cat strolls proudly in his handsome white shoes . . . until he steps into a pile of strawberries. Oh, no! Does Pete cry? Goodness, no! Instead, the unflappable feline struts along in his newly red shoes . . . until he steps into some blueberries, a mud puddle, and a bucket of water. The opportunity for preschoolers to interact and respond during a read-aloud is irresistible. They will call out the new colors of Pete's shoes and exclaim, "Goodness, no!" Look up Pete's song on the author's website or YouTube before your reading, and expect to hear pleas to "read it again!" along with *Pete the Cat and His Four Groovy Buttons* (2012), a Geisel Honor Book, and *Pete the Cat Saves Christmas* (2012).

Pete the Cat: Pete the Cat and His Four Groovy Buttons
(Pete the Cat series)

By Eric Litwin. Illus. by James Dean. HarperCollins, 2012. 32p. Ages 4-8

A backward-counting exercise is cleverly hidden in this picture book that's perfect for beginning readers: Pete has four buttons on his shirt, then one pops off, then two, and so on until the only button he has left is his belly button. The scruffy feline has become a popular and familiar character and, once again, there's a song to download that he sings as he loses his buttons one by one. GEISEL HONOR BOOK

Pete the Cat: Pete the Cat Saves Christmas
(Pete the Cat series)
By Eric Litwin. Illus. by James Dean. HarperCollins, 2012. 32p. Ages 4-8

Lots of popular series end up with a Christmas-themed volume, and this one is no exception. Borrowing from the "helping Santa" pantheon of children's media, this has Pete travel up from Key West in a van when Santa Cat gets sick. But does anyone have a present for Pete?

Please Take Me for a Walk
By Susan Gal. Illus. by the author. Knopf, 2010. 40p. Ages 3-7

An exuberant black-and-white puppy wants to go for a walk, and he's eager to give many reasons why. With simple, descriptive text and a nicely balanced use of the repeated phrase "please take me for a walk," this will have readers enthused about exploring their own communities. Expressive, mixed-media illustrations enhance the story that takes young readers on a trip to explore a friendly neighborhood through the protagonist's eyes.

The Pout-Pout Fish in the Big-Big Dark
By Deborah Diesen. Illus. by Dan Hanna. Farrar, 2010. 32p. Ages 2-5

Ms. Clam yawns and her pearl is carried away by an ocean current. Mr. Fish is determined to find the "yawn-gone pearl." Afraid of the dark, his heart "flit-fluttered" as he swam in the "heap-deep black" near the ocean floor, and he almost gives up the search until Miss Shimmer appears and supportively swims at his side. With Mr. Lantern's help they find the pearl and return to celebrate the power of friendship, which is "Always big, BIG, BIGGER / Than the dark." Whimsically detailed cartoon illustrations of the ocean invite repeated viewings and support repeated listenings of the playful, poetic text.

Press Here
By Hervé Tullet. Illus. by the author. Chronicle, 2011. 56p. Ages 3-7

Press on one yellow dot, turn the page, and it becomes two dots. Rub a dot and yellow turns to red. Shake the book to scatter dots. This inventive interactive book uses no technology, just expertly planned page-turns and the reader's imagination. The painted colored dots are set against generous white space, making transitions easy to follow and anticipate. Words engage playfully, anticipating curiosity and surprise at each cause-and-effect sequence. Whether shared with groups or one-on-one, the answer to the book's final question—"Want to do it all over again?"—will surely be . . . "Yes!"

Purple Little Bird

By Greg Foley. Illus. by the author. HarperCollins/Balzer + Bray, 2011. 32p. Ages 3-6

Purple Little Bird keeps a perfectly purple-colored home, from fence to garden to walls. But something is missing. Purple Little Bird ventures out and sees Brown Bear's cave in the green forest, Gray Goat's snowy perch on a cliff, Yellow Camel's dusty desert, and Blue Frog's refreshing pond. None of these places make exactly perfect homes for Purple Little Bird, but he now realizes that what his home really needs is a fresh, multicolored palette. This is an appealing selection for storytimes about colors, creativity, and even as part of an introduction to different ecologies.

Puss in Boots

By Jerry Pinkney. Illus. by the author. Dial, 2012. 40p. Ages 4-8

This faithful-to-the-original version of Charles Perrault's classic fairy tale is set in France around the early eighteenth century. Puss, a clever black, white, and silver shorthair tabby cat, uses trickery to win for his penniless young master a fortune and the hand of a princess. Elaborate illustrations rendered in graphite, colored pencil, and watercolors feature lavish costumes and detailed settings.

Question Boy Meets Little Miss Know-It-All

By Peter Catalonotto. Illus. by the author. Simon & Schuster/Atheneum, 2012. 40p. Ages 5-7

Kids may recognize themselves, or more likely each other, in these two characters; everyone knows someone just like one of these two. The friendly competition goes back and forth until Question Boy trumps all answers with the ultimate question: "Why?" Realistic watercolors portray the two friends in close-up, putting this just enough in your face.

The Quiet Book

By Deborah Underwood. Illus. by Renata Liwska. Houghton Mifflin Harcourt, 2010. 32p. Ages 3-5

Quiet isn't only reserved for bedtime. Listening to birdsong, sharing secrets, or making wishes are all everyday occasions celebrated by a gentle hush. Muted earth tones and soft pencil sketches aptly portray a loveable cast of characters as they make their way through an ordinary day. Discover the quiet anticipation of waiting atop a roller coaster. Revel in the comfortable silence shared between two best friends. Savor the soundless joy of a lollipop. And when you're done relaxing, visit *The Loud Book* (2011), listed earlier in this chapter.

The Quiet Place

By Sarah Stewart. Illus. by David Small. Farrar/Margaret Ferguson, 2012. 40p. Ages 6-8

The "quiet place" here refers to a sanctuary young Isabel builds for herself out of a cardboard moving box after her family emigrates from Mexico to Michigan. She decorates the inside and spends time there by herself, often writing letters to her beloved aunt left behind. Immigration stories resonate with an increasing number of young readers, and the end, in which the quiet place isn't so quiet with the addition of new friends, satisfies.

The Rabbit Problem

By Emily Gravett. Illus. by the author. Simon & Schuster, 2010. 32p. Ages 4-8

This playful take on a mathematical problem posed by Fibonacci in the thirteenth century illustrates what could happen if two healthy rabbits left in a field for a year grew a family. Based on the famous, eponymous number sequence, this 12-month story chronicles population growth of a very furry nature. In addition to multiplying rabbits, the humorous depiction of seasonal woes (sunburned bunnies) and agricultural dilemmas (carrot under/overabundance) adds appeal. The clever calendar layout and paper enclosures make this a pleasure to read again and again.

Rah, Rah, Radishes! A Vegetable Chant

By April Pulley Sayre. Illus. by the author. Simon & Schuster/Beach Lane, 2011. 32p. Ages 3-6

Celebrate vegetables in all their fresh glory! Bold color photos depict a fetching array of bushels, baskets, and piles of fresh vegetables, many familiar (celery, tomatoes, carrots) and others not so (rutabaga, fennel, kohlrabi). The text begs to be read in a cheerleading rhythm: "Oh boy, bok choy! Brussels sprout. Broccoli. Cauliflower. Shout it out!" Good nutrition should be this fun. Share this title at storytimes or in class units about healthful eating, gardening, farmers markets, or harvest.

Ready, Set, 100th Day!

By Nancy Elizabeth Wallace. Illus. by the author. Marshall Cavendish, 2011. 32p. Ages 4-8

One hundredth–day celebrations are a staple in early childhood class-rooms, and books on the topic abound. This one appeals, with cut paper illustrations and photos that clearly show appropriate ways to come up with the number one hundred: ten differently shaped paper punches to make ten groups of ten, five different pom-poms to make five groups of twenty, and so on. Skip counting and grouping is taught in the early grades; this makes math more fun.

The Red Hen

By Ed Emberley. Illus. by Rebecca Emberley. Roaring Brook/Neal Porter, 2010. 32p. Ages 3-6

In this simple, contemporary telling of the familiar tale, a hen discovers a cake recipe and asks the dog, rat, and frog to help mix, bake, and frost as unnamed chicks flit in the background. The vibrant paper characters sporting eye-popping features are presented in humorous, changing poses and perspectives amid baking utensils and ingredients. This book is likely to prompt humorous reader/listener conversations, requests for repeated readings, puppet making, and storytelling. A concluding cake recipe sweetens the fun to further extend the story.

Red Knit Cap Girl

By Naoko Stoop. Illus. by the author. Little, Brown, 2012. 40p. Ages 3-6

Many children have an innate appreciation of the natural world, and so does the Red Knit Cap Girl. She enjoys quiet and is comfortable in her solitude; however, she aspires to speak with the Moon and seeks help from her animal friends (a white bunny, bear, squirrel, hedgehog, and owl). This gentle story is beautifully interpreted with textured illustrations of greens, blues, yellows, and reds, created in pencil, acrylic, and ink on plywood. The satisfying ending and Zen-like lesson make this a good bedtime choice.

See Me Run

By Paul Meisel. Illus. by the author. Holiday, 2011. 32p. Ages 4-8

In this easy-to-read picture book, after a dog leads his canine companions in a playful romp through the park, the dogs start digging and uncover a skeletal surprise! The text uses short familiar words and sentences as well as repetition to build reading skills and comprehension. Children will enjoy the humorous pictures, which depict a variety of dog breeds. GEISEL HONOR BOOK

Shadow

By Suzy Lee. Illus. by the author. Chronicle, 2010. 40p. Ages 4-8

Black-and-white charcoal art highlighted in yellow effectively "tell" this story of a clever young girl who discovers, and plays with, shadows in the attic. Some of the shadows are friendly, some less so, and she must make all end well before dinner in this imaginative adventure.

Shark vs. Train

By Chris Barton. Illus. by Tom Lichtenheld. Little, Brown, 2010. 40p. Ages 4-6

This hilarious match-up features two kid-favorite toys pitted against one another in settings that favor one (a lemonade stand is too watery under the ocean) over the other (trains aren't good at diving off high boards), and sometimes neither (a lack of opposable thumbs hampers video-game playing for both). Puns add to the humor ("I'm going to 'choo-choo' you up!"), and young readers will eagerly await the next contest.

Shoe-la-la!

By Karen Beaumont. Illus. by LeUyen Pham. Scholastic, 2011. 40p. Ages 2-5

Four young friends search for the perfect shoes to wear to a party. With no parent in sight they scurry to the Shoe-la-la store, where an elegant salesman helps them try on all kinds of shoes he names in a rhythmic litany. The girls leave empty handed as the exhausted salesman is surrounded by hundreds of shoes. At home they decorate their own shoes for the party. The perky text combined with appealing illustrations of a multicultural cast amid richly detailed home and retail settings invite repeated readings.

A Sick Day for Amos McGee

By Philip C. Stead. Illus. by Erin E. Stead. Roaring Brook/Neal Porter, 2010. 32p. Ages 2-6

Amos McGee is a zookeeper who always has time to visit his friends. The elephant, the tortoise, the penguin, the rhinoceros, and the owl all wait patiently each day for him to stop and visit. But one day, Amos is not there, and it is up to his friends to discover why. All it will take is a very special bus ride across town. The spare, gently humorous story, pairs well with the richly detailed yet understated illustrations. Young readers connect immediately, not just with Amos but with all his zoo friends as well. CALDECOTT MEDAL

Sky Color

By Peter H. Reynolds. Illus. by the author. Candlewick, 2012. 32p. Ages 4-8

How is Marisol going to paint the sky in a mural for her school's library, when there is no blue paint available? Creativity is on display as the budding artist, known for her unusual clothes, artsy possessions, and her belief that everyone can be an artist, comes up with her own solution to use a combination of colors to replicate the complex true color of the sky in real life. This inspiring story encourages young readers and artists to explore their creativity, imagination, critical thinking, and problem-solving skills.

Sleep like a Tiger

By Mary Logue. Illus. by Pamela Zagarenski. Houghton Mifflin Harcourt, 2012. 34p. Ages 4-6

The perennial issue of bedtime procrastination is soothingly and imaginatively addressed here as a young girl, reluctant to go to bed, is told by her parents that she doesn't have to, but she has to get in her pajamas; she doesn't have to go to sleep, but she has to get into the bed; and so on. She asks about a litany of other animals' bedtime routines, finally curling up like a tiger herself and yielding naturally to her own sleepiness. Detailed, whimsical mixed-media artwork supplements the comforting text. CALDECOTT HONOR BOOK

Solomon Crocodile

By Catherine Rayner. Illus. by the author. Farrar, 2011. 32p. Ages 3-7

Rambunctious kids will sympathize with Solomon, whose antics are not appreciated by the other animals living in his river. He doesn't really mind, though, until the hippo kicks him out. Soon, though, he finds a partner in crime: an even peskier crocodile. Childlike artwork in scratchy black outline brings the swampy setting to life.

Spike the Mixed-Up Monster

By Susan Hood. Illus. by Melissa Sweet. Simon & Schuster/Paula Wiseman, 2012. 40p. (DC) Ages 4-7

This very well may be a child's first introduction to the *axolotl*, a kind of salamander found in Mexico. Spike spends hours at the lake earnestly practicing his fiercest monster moves but because he's so small, the other animals find him more adorable than fearsome. But it's Spike alone who stands up to a Gila monster . . . and ends up making a new friend. Basic words and animal names in Spanish are peppered throughout the story, with supplemental matter featuring photographs and information about "Spike and his *amigos*," plus a Spanish glossary.

Squeak, Rumble, Whomp! Whomp! Whomp! A Sonic Adventure

By Wynton Marsalis. Illus. by Paul Rogers. Candlewick, 2012. 32p. (DC) Ages 2-7

A young, trumpet-playing African American boy takes readers on a delightful auditory tour of his New Orleans home and neighborhood, highlighting the wide variety of sounds he hears throughout the day. Sounds from doors, trucks, instruments, clocks, musicians, and all sorts of places make music to his ears. Featuring a rhythmic and rhyming text and lively illustrations, this makes it fun to compare and contrast the sounds of musical instruments with the sounds of everyday life in a home or neighborhood.

Summer Jackson: Grown Up

By Teresa E. Harris. Illus. by A. G. Ford. HarperCollins/Katherine Tegen, 2011. 32p. (DC) Ages 5-8

Summer Jackson, a high-spirited and precocious African American girl, can't wait to grow up. She decides to wear a blazer and high heels to mimic her professional mother, a consultant, and soon begins charging kids at school for her services. When Summer's parents reverse roles by acting like children, leaving adult responsibilities to her, Summer decides that being a seven-year-old is much easier. The humorous story, animated illustrations, and spunky character charm.

Suppose You Meet a Dinosaur: A First Book of Manners

By Judy Sierra. Illus. by Tim Bowers. Knopf, 2012. 40p. Ages 4-7

This is similar in premise to the How Do Dinosaurs . . . series, but young kids won't mind that; they'll simply appreciate the silliness as a little girl and her not-too-scary dinosaur friend learn how to be polite to one another as they do the grocery shopping. The signature terms, "Please," "Thank you," "Excuse me," and so on, are in big, bold text to reinforce the message.

Ten Rules You Absolutely Must Not Break If You Want to Survive the School Bus

By John Grandits. Illus. by Michael Allen Austin. Clarion, 2011. 32p. Ages 5-8

Kyle is so nervous that he is dreading his first trip aboard the school bus. His older brother James explains that riding the school bus is not an easy process—there are secret survival skills (rules) related to seat location, eye contact, girls, touching other kids' stuff, big kids, the bus bully, and so on that must not be broken. Large full-page acrylic paint illustrations brilliantly capture Kyle's fear and trepidations, even as he breaks all the rules. In the end, Kyle not only survives but adds rule eleven: "Never, absolutely never, pay attention to your big brother's list."

There's Going to Be a Baby

By John Burningham. Illus. by Helen Oxenbury. Candlewick, 2010. 48p. Ages 2-5

When a young son is told, "There's going to be a baby," he asks the usual questions, but he also has personal questions for his mother. This husband-and-wife author and illustrator team answers these questions with grace and style. During her pregnancy, the mother and son visit a restaurant, museum, garden, zoo, beach, bank, and the doctor. The boy imagines his sibling working in each establishment and then expresses a good thought, such as ". . . looking after the animals," and then a not-so-good thought, such as "The baby might get eaten by a tiger." The colors and softness of the illustrations strengthen the mother's calm and safe replies.

This Is Not My Hat

By Jon Klassen. Illus. by the author. Candlewick, 2012. 40p. Ages 4-7

This nearly wordless book's sly humor comes through in the art, which almost directly contradicts everything that's stated in the text. A small fish is certain the large fish, who previously owned the small hat the small fish stole, either won't notice it's gone, won't know who took it, or won't know where the thief is hiding. Dark colors emphasize the sinister comedy, suitable for slightly older readers than the simple text might imply. CALDECOTT MEDAL

Three by the Sea

By Mini Grey. Illus. by the author. Knopf, 2011. 32p. Ages 5-7

Dog, Cat, and Mouse are living together happily by the sea when a mysterious stranger arrives and stirs up trouble. With new ideas about everything, will he convince the threesome that their comfortable lives are not so happy? Is Cat cleaning house or napping? Why can't Mouse cook something without cheese? And wouldn't the garden be better with more than just Dog's bones? Humor and a charming text work well with colorful, endearing illustrations to explore the nature of friendship and cooperation.

Three Little Pigs: An Architectural Tale

By Steven Guarnaccia. Illus. by the author. Abrams, 2010. 32p. Ages 4-8

This contemporary retelling showcases the works of noted architects Frank Gehry, Philip Johnson, and Frank Lloyd Wright in the guise of three pigs: "Gehry" lives in a house of scraps; "Johnson" in a house of glass, of course; and "Wright" in the brick house, Fallingwater itself. The wolf himself is up-to-date as well, sporting a leather jacket and shades and riding in on a motorcycle.

Thunder Birds: Nature's Flying Predators

By Jim Arnosky. Illus. by the author. Sterling, 2011. 32p. Ages 8-11

Fascinating details of predatory birds come to life in this eye-catching informational book, from the eighty-inch wingspan that aids the head-first swoops of the Brown Pelican to the four wide toes that help the Great White Heron balance deftly in mud. Dramatic acrylic paintings feature multiple life-size depictions of birds and several fold-out pages add to the visual appeal. Arnosky combines fascinating facts with anecdotes from his own experiences, making this an excellent choice for students, browsers, and anyone enthralled by the natural world.

Tía Isa Wants a Car

By Meg Medina. Illus. by Claudio Muñoz. Candlewick, 2011. 32p. (DC) Ages 4-7

Tía Isa is determined to get a car to take her family—her whole family, including those members still waiting to come to America—to the beach. The endearing, unnamed narrator moves the story along by asking questions about what type of car Tía Isa will choose. By working secret small jobs in her neighborhood, the narrator saves up enough to help, but will it be enough? This endearing story, illustrated with pencil, ink, and watercolor, has universal appeal, though readers familiar with the immigrant experience may be especially moved.

Toads on Toast
By Linda Bailey. Illus. by Colin Jack. Kids Can, 2012. 32p. Ages 3-7

Eeeeew! Toads on toast? Fortunately, resourceful Mamma Toad has an alternate recipe for fox to make: Toad-in-a-Hole, which some kids may already know means an egg cooked in a piece of toast (no toads!). Cartoon-style artwork outlined in scratchy black fits the energetic text well, and a Toad-in-a-Hole recipe is included.

The Tooth Fairy Meets El Ratón Pérez
By René Colato Laínez. Illus. by Tom Lintern. Tricycle, 2010. 32p. (DC) Ages 5-7

The Tooth Fairy meets her Mexican counterpart, El Ratón Pérez, in this story of their rivalry over Mexican American Miguelito's lost tooth. The snappy dialogue includes exclamations in both English and Spanish, and the message about the power of cooperation is neatly masked in this lively story.

Tuck Me In
By Dean Hacohen. Illus. by Sherry Scharschmidt. Candlewick, 2010. 40p. Ages 1-4

Who needs to be tucked in at night? Everyone from a cozy piglet to a colorful baby peacock in this playful bedtime tale for the youngest listeners. Each infant animal responds with an enthusiastic "I do!," setting the stage for a gentle turn of a half-page that neatly covers the youngster with a patterned blanket. Whether the adult reader turns the page or the toddler does the covering up, the endearing animal illustrations and clever page engineering provide a perfect lead-in for a toddler's own time for tucking in.

Tweak Tweak
By Eve Bunting. Illus. by Sergio Ruzzier. Clarion, 2011. 40p. Ages 2-5

Mama Elephant takes Little Elephant for a walk, directing her daughter to tweak her tail twice if she has questions. Little Elephant is curious, and it is not long before the first "tweak, tweak!" Observing a frog, Little Elephant wants to know if she can jump like one. Mama explains that elephants do not jump, but they can stomp and make a big sound. This pattern repeats throughout their walk. By the end, Little Elephant identifies many things she cannot do, but also recognizes how she will become a "big, strong, smart, beautiful elephant" just like her mother.

Under Ground

By Denise Fleming. Illus. by the author. Simon & Schuster/Beach Lane, 2012. 40p. Ages 2-5

This introduction to what happens under the ground opens with a bird's-eye view, then goes below to reveal where gardens begin their growth and many creatures nest. The simple, rhythmic text brings the earthy setting to life for the youngest readers and listeners, and colorful textured pulp illustrations evoke the grainy feel of the "underground."

Underground

By Shane W. Evans. Illus. by the author. Roaring Brook/Neal Porter, 2011. 32p. (DC) Ages 4-8

It's not easy to make challenging subjects such as slavery and the Underground Railroad accessible to very young readers without compromising the severe reality of the experience, but text and art work exceptionally well here to do just that. Dark, somber illustrations keep tension high and focus on the journey, which includes death, fear, and exhaustion. As the escapees progress, there is a growing light in the distance, and as dawn breaks in a series of stunning full-page spreads in bright gold, they finally reach freedom. CORETTA SCOTT KING ILLUSTRATOR AWARD

Village Garage

By G. Brian Karas. Illus. by the author. Holt/Christy Ottaviano, 2010. 32p. Ages 4-8

Seasons in a New England town are depicted through the workers and machinery at the village garage. A dump truck and wood chipper are used for spring clean-up. In the summer, mowers cut grass and the front loader gives rides for the Fourth of July. The elephant machine vacuums leaves in the fall and hand tools fix leaky pipes. Workers and plows wait for the first winter snowfall. Minimal text humorously conveys some of the action, and young listeners will pore over the distinctive, richly detailed pages to view activities of machinery and multicultural characters on center stage and in the background.

What's Special about Me, Mama?

By Kristina Evans. Illus. by Javaka Steptoe. Disney/Jump at the Sun, 2011. 32p. (DC) Ages 3-6

An African American child who has eyes, ears, hair, skin tone, and other physical features that resemble those of other members of his family wants to know what is truly special and unique about *him*. His patient and loving mom explains that what makes him special is her love for him. Detailed collage illustrations aptly portray the emotions and love shared by Mama and her son.

When a Dragon Moves In

By Jodi Moore. Illus. by Howard McWilliam. Flashlight, 2011. 32p. Ages 4-7

A boy and a dragon make friends when the dragon moves into the boy's sandcastle, and at first everything's fine: He plays Frisbee with the dragon, delights in the dragon's bubbles and smoke rings, and floats on the dragon's stomach. The dragon protects the sandcastle from bullies. But after the dragon eats his sister's sandwiches, claws the brownies, and sprays his sister with sand, the boy tells the dragon to move out. This celebration of the imagination offers gentle lessons in manners too.

Where's My T-R-U-C-K?

By Karen Beaumont. Illus. by David Catrow. Dial, 2011. 32p. Ages 3-6

Tommy is mad because he has lost his T-R-U-C-K and all the alternatives and distractions offered and suggested by mom, dad, sis, and grandma make no difference to Tommy—all he wants is his T-R-U-C-K! Bowser, the family dog, is seen running away with something in his mouth on every page spread. The drama ends when Tommy finds his T-R-U-C-K buried in a giant hole that Bowser's dug. The drama of the lost T-R-U-C-K is documented in a rhyming text that is entertaining, descriptive, and hilarious. The bright and bold full-page pencil and watercolor illustrations along with the repetitive T-R-U-C-K make this great to read aloud.

Where's Walrus?

By Stephen Savage. Illus. by the author. Scholastic, 2011. 32p. Ages 3-7

This wordless picture book follows Walrus's adventures as he escapes from the zoo and embarks on an ever more fanciful tour of the city. With the bumbling zookeeper always one step behind, Walrus spends a day exploring and posing with many different people, including a mannequin, a caricature artist, and a cabaret dancer. It is as a diver, however, that he really makes his splash! Each page is filled to the edge with bold, simple lines and colors and drips with humor.

Who Built the Stable? A Nativity Poem

By Ashley Bryan. Illus. by the author. Simon & Schuster/Atheneum, 2012. 34p. Ages 4-8

Richly colorful paintings with the look of stained glass illuminate this Nativity story portrayed in an African jungle setting. A young boy is the central character here, making the Nativity story relevant and immediate to contemporary kids. He is apprenticed to his father, a carpenter, and builds the stable himself to offer shelter to the Holy Family.

Wumbers: It's Words Cre8ted with Numbers

By Amy Krouse Rosenthal. Illus. by Tom Lichtenheld. Chronicle, 2012. 40p. Ages 6-8

What do you get when you combine a word and a number? A wumber! Here, sentences made up of words contain numbers in place of letters with similar sounds. Each two-page spread is a discrete unit portraying a variety of familiar childhood settings: forts ("I like 10ts, 2!"), a tea party ("We have the 2na salad and the pl8s"), and the like. Colorful cartoon illustrations provide a visual hint for young readers who may have difficulty with some of the wumbers. There's no d9ing that this gr8 book will inspire kids to create their own wumber situations.

You Can Be a Friend

By Tony Dungy and Lauren Dungy. Illus. by Ron Mazellan. Simon & Schuster/Little Simon Inspirations, 2011. 32p. (DC) Ages 4-7

The overt message here may be a bit preachy, but its transparency is also its appeal: this is a straightforward demonstration of the virtue of friendship and tolerance, featuring a multicultural cast and a main character in a wheelchair. The fact that one of the authors is a retired Super Bowl–winning NFL coach adds to its appeal.

You're Finally Here!

By Melanie Watt. Illus. by the author. Disney/Hyperion, 2011. 40p. Ages 3-6

"You're finally here!" Rabbit exclaims as you, the reader, finally open his book and turn the pages. All is joy and celebration until Rabbit stops to demand, "Where were you?" Rabbit wants to make sure you know how unfair, how annoying, how boring, and how rude it was to make him wait . . . until he gets a call on his cell phone. This story has instant appeal at school visits and outreach events. Kids will laugh as the dramatically moody Rabbit swings from ecstatic to sulky and back again.

Z Is for Moose

By Kelly Bingham. Illus. by Paul O. Zelinsky. Greenwillow, 2012. 32p. Ages 3-7

Zebra figures he's stage-directing a straightforward alphabet play, but he hasn't accounted for Moose, his spotlight-seeking friend. Moose first tries to muscle in on Duck, who's representing the letter "D." He then continues upstaging the presentation, jumping into the ice cream for the letter "I" and popping into a kangaroo's pouch for the letter "K." But Moose is in for a surprise: this time, "M" is for mouse, not moose. Of course, Moose throws a tantrum through the rest of the alphabet until Zebra gives in and lets Moose have the last letter: "Z is for Zebra's friend, Moose."

Early Readers

Recommendations for cultivating a diverse collection are indicated by "(DC)."

Babymouse: A Very Babymouse Christmas
(Babymouse series)

By Jennifer L. Holm and Matthew Holm. Illus. by Jennifer L. Holm. Random, 2011. 96p.

Ages 8-10

Opening with a slightly adapted version of the famous poem "...not a creature was stirring, not even a ... BABYMOUSE!" coupled with an image that shows Babymouse's empty bed, the fifteenth title in this popular series features Babymouse meeting a mall Santa, celebrating Hanukkah with a friend, and hoping for the hot gift of the year, a "Whiz-Bang."

Babymouse: Babymouse Burns Rubber
(Babymouse series)

By Jennifer L. Holm and Matthew Holm. Illus. by Jennifer L. Holm. Random, 2010. 96p.

Ages 8-10

Babymouse puts paw to metal in the twelfth installment of the popular series, in which Babymouse takes on soapbox racing. Engaging illustrations combine with loveable characters to create memorable stories, and the clever word play makes pop culture references. The *Goodnight Moon* spoof is especially delicious: "Goodnight math homework that's not finished. Goodnight stinky gym socks." Another checkered flag for Babymouse! Other hits include *Cupcake Tycoon* (2010), *Mad Scientist* (2011), *A Very Babymouse Christmas* (2011), and *Babymouse for President* (2012).

Babymouse: Babymouse for President
(Babymouse series)

By Jennifer L. Holm and Matthew Holm. Illus. by Jennifer L. Holm. Random, 2012. 96p. Ages 8-10

Published just in time for the 2012 election for the President of the United States, this gives early readers of graphic novels their own take on a presidential election. This time, the opening scene features a convention hall, "Babymouse Campaign Headquarters," as her election is announced, but readers (and Babymouse) are quickly brought back down to earth when it becomes clear this is all in her imagination, and in reality, she's facing the coach, who chides her for forgetting her sneakers, again. Babymouse can't get rid of the presidential bug, especially when she sees the student council president posters and envisions herself behind the big desk, outlawing homework, improving cafeteria food, and so on.

Babymouse: Cupcake Tycoon
(Babymouse series)

By Jennifer L. Holm and Matthew Holm. Illus. by Jennifer L. Holm. Random, 2010. 96p. Ages 8-10

This library-themed entry in the popular Babymouse series gives Babymouse's ambitions a way to shine: After she accidentally sets off the fire alarm sprinklers in the library, Babymouse must come up with an entrepreneurial way to earn money to replace the damaged books. How better than a cupcake sale? Of course, it wouldn't hurt to win grand prize in the fundraising competition to boot.

Babymouse: Mad Scientist
(Babymouse series)

By Jennifer L. Holm and Matthew Holm. Illus. by Jennifer L. Holm. Random, 2011. 96p. Ages 8-10

As always, Babymouse has grand ambitions. This time, the science fair is coming up, and she envisions herself winning the Nobel Prize and daydreams about science fiction movies. Once she starts to work in earnest, she discovers a new character: Squish the Amoeba, whose bright green contrasts with the sugary pink tone of the rest of the Babymouse series. Will Squish be enough to earn her first prize?

Benny and Penny: Benny and Penny in Lights Out
(Benny and Penny series)

By Geoffrey Hayes. Illus. by the author. RAW Junior/Toon, 2012. 32p. Ages 5-7

It's time for Benny and his little sister Penny to go to bed, but Benny's just not ready. Penny acts as his conscience here, telling him, "It's time to brush our teeth!" and "You need to get under the covers! It's quiet time!" and generally trying to keep him on track, which doesn't work. He peeks out the window, claims pirates have stolen the moon, scares Penny in the bathroom by turning out the lights and making a face illuminated by his flashlight, and eventually, even goes outside to find his pirate hat. Once again, the antics are true to life, the dialogue realistic, and the pale graphic artwork is child friendly and accessible to early readers.

Benny and Penny: Benny and Penny in the Toy Breaker
(Benny and Penny series)

By Geoffrey Hayes. Illus. by the author. RAW Junior/Toon, 2010. 32p. Ages 5-7

Mouse siblings Benny and Penny hide their toys when Cousin Bo visits because he breaks their toys whenever he plays with them. When they go on a treasure hunt to find backyard "loot," Benny and Penny try to avoid Bo, but he won't stop pestering them. The cartoon panels provide a good balance between information shown in the pictures and spelled out in the ballooned dialogue. This enjoyable introduction to reading—and to reading comics—is accessible for beginning readers and continued in *Benny and Penny in Lights Out* (2012).

Bink & Gollie

By Kate DiCamillo and Alison McGee. Illus. by Tony Fucile. Candlewick, 2010. 96p. Ages 6-10

Short, easy-to-read chapters and comic pencil-and-ink illustrations make these relatable stories accessible and laugh-out-loud fun. Best friends Bink and Gollie may be complete opposites; but opposites attract as they negotiate the vicissitudes of friendship in three separate stories that are accessible and appealing to new readers. GEISEL AWARD

Cat the Cat: Let's Say Hi to Friends Who Fly!
(Cat the Cat series)

By Mo Willems. Illus. by the author. HarperCollins/Balzer + Bray, 2010. 32p. Ages 2–5

This combination friendship story and concept book about which animals fly is accessibly portrayed in Willems's trademark kid-friendly style, following on the introduction to Cat the Cat in *Cat the Cat: Who Is That?* (2010). Here, Cat the Cat meets playground friends who fly, including Bee the Bee, Bird the Bird, and Bat the Bat. But can Rhino fly? You bet—on an airplane!

Cat the Cat: Time to Sleep, Sheep the Sheep!
(Cat the Cat series)

By Mo Willems. Illus. by the author. HarperCollins/Balzer + Bray, 2010. 32p. Ages 2–5

This time, Cat the Cat and fellow critters Pig the Pig, Crab the Crab, and more get ready for bed. The litany of prebedtime activities will be familiar to kids just learning to connect their daily activities to written words on a page.

Cat the Cat: What's Your Sound, Hound the Hound?
(Cat the Cat series)

By Mo Willems. Illus. by the author. HarperCollins/Balzer + Bray, 2010. 32p. Ages 2–5

Similar to *Cat the Cat: Let's Say Hi to Friends Who Fly!* (2010), this also presents a concept in the context of an easy-to-read friendship story. This time, the concept is animal sounds, from a dog, to a chick, to a . . . bunny?

Cat the Cat: Who Is That?
(Cat the Cat series)

By Mo Willems. Illus. by the author. HarperCollins/Balzer + Bray, 2010. 32p. Ages 2–5

Cat the Cat greets her many friends—Mouse the Mouse, Duck the Duck, Fish the Fish—and introduces them to readers as she answers the repeated question, "Cat the Cat, who is that?" When she meets a strange looking alien who's building a tower of blocks, she lets out a surprised "EEP!" and can only say "I have NO idea" when asked, "Cat the Cat, who is that?" When the alien waves to her and says, "Blarggie! Blarggie!," Cat the Cat realizes she's found a new friend. Most of the words are sight words or are easily decoded and appear in large bold type well suited for children just beginning to read on their own. Additional series favorites include *Let's Say Hi to Friends Who Fly!* (2010), *Time to Sleep, Sheep the Sheep!* (2010), and *What's Your Sound, Hound the Hound?* (2010).

Dodsworth: Dodsworth in Rome
(Dodsworth Books series)

By Tim Egan. Illus. by the author. Houghton Mifflin Harcourt, 2011. 48p. Ages 4-7

That peripatetic mouse named Dodsworth and his friend the duck are on the road again! This time, they head to Rome, where Dodsworth and the duck sample the gelato, drive a scooter in the Eternal City's fabled traffic, and win a pizza dough–throwing contest. Much of the book's comedy derives from the duck's literal-mindedness, reminiscent of Amelia Bedelia. It's just the type of broad humor that young readers love and adults also can appreciate. Children who like this book should try the other Dodsworth books and also check out the picture book that opened the series, *The Pink Refrigerator* (2007).

Elephant & Piggie: Can I Play Too?
(Elephant & Piggie series)

By Mo Willems. Illus. by the author. Disney/Hyperion, 2010. 64p. Ages 3-6

The theme of friendship is strong in all Elephant & Piggie titles but is explicitly addressed here when the two best friends try to include someone who isn't quite like them: a snake who wishes to play catch. In trademark imaginative fashion, the three come up with a new way to play together that includes everyone.

Elephant & Piggie: Happy Pig Day!
(Elephant & Piggie series)

By Mo Willems. Illus. by the author. Disney/Hyperion, 2011. 64p. Ages 3-6

Who knew there was such a holiday as Happy Pig Day? Gerald didn't, and now that the celebrations have begun he's feeling a bit left out. Young readers who might not be able to articulate why they do or do not feel included in a particular holiday will nevertheless empathize with the emotions here and will be as relieved as Gerald to learn that Happy Pig Day is not just for pigs—it is also for those who love pigs.

Elephant & Piggie: I Am Going!
(Elephant & Piggie series)

By Mo Willems. Illus. by the author. Disney/Hyperion, 2010. 64p. Ages 3-6

Gerald and Piggie's contrasting personalities are on humorous display here when Piggie's carefree decision to go have lunch sends anxious Gerald into a tailspin. Young kids still learning to cope with challenges will recognize Gerald's panic as he wonders who he will skip with, who he will wear a funny hat with, and more; his relief is palpable when he learns the reason for Piggie's departure and the two sit down to share a "big" lunch.

Elephant & Piggie: I Broke My Trunk!
(Elephant & Piggie series)

By Mo Willems. Illus. by the author. Disney/Hyperion, 2011. 64p. Ages 3-6

It's hard to say which is the funniest title in the Elephant & Piggie series, but this one definitely contends. Elephant tells a progressively sillier tale about how he broke his trunk, beginning with an attempt to lift Hippo up in the air with his trunk, culminating with lifting up Hippo's sister AND her piano. But none of those things actually broke his trunk; his trunk broke when he tripped and fell in his eagerness to tell the story to his best friend, Piggie. GEISEL HONOR BOOK

Elephant & Piggie: Let's Go for a Drive!
(Elephant & Piggie series)

By Mo Willems. Illus. by the author. Disney/Hyperion, 2012. 64p. Ages 3-6

Anyone who's tried to go on an outing with young kids in tow will recognize the litany of "necessary" items and reasons to go back into the house to fetch things. Gerald worries about all the things they need, such as suitcases, a map, and more, and Piggie provides them; the two are only a little stymied when they realize they don't have a car. GEISEL HONOR BOOK

Elephant & Piggie: Listen to My Trumpet!
(Elephant & Piggie series)

By Mo Willems. Illus. by the author. Disney/Hyperion, 2012. 64p. Ages 3-6

Piggie's devil-may-care attitude, big dreams, and healthy self-esteem come to the fore when she displays her trumpet-playing "talent" for Gerald and expects appropriate affirmation. Gerald knows what he has to say but takes some time to muster up his courage to reveal to his best friend that "that is not music." Of course, Piggie isn't dismayed by this; actually, she was trying to sound like an elephant!

Elephant & Piggie: Should I Share My Ice Cream?
(Elephant & Piggie series)
By Mo Willems. Illus. by the author. Disney/Hyperion, 2011. 64p. Ages 3–6
Worrywart Gerald is prone to overthink things, and this time is no exception. He can't wait to eat his delicious ice cream, but he worries about whether or not he should share such a delicious treat with his best friend. But what if she doesn't like this flavor? Alert readers will sense what's about to happen, recognizing you can't wait too long to eat ice cream.

Elephant & Piggie: We Are in a Book!
(Elephant & Piggie series)
By Mo Willems. Illus. by the author. Disney/Hyperion, 2010. 64p. Ages 3–6
Kid-favorite characters Gerald the elephant and Piggie the pig are back and discover a wonderful thing: they are in a book, and they are being read! Things only get more exciting when they realize they can make the reader say a funny word such as . . . "Banana!" However, Gerald's joy turns to shock when he learns that all books end, even the one he is in. It's up to Piggie to figure out a way to keep the story going. With only a few words per page, books in this series are intended for children just learning to read but are fun for all. Numbering nearly twenty, recent titles include *I Am Going!* (2010), *Can I Play Too?* (2010), *Should I Share My Ice Cream?* (2011), *I Broke My Trunk!* (2011), *Happy Pig Day!* (2011), *Listen to My Trumpet!* (2012), and *Let's Go for a Drive!* (2012). GEISEL HONOR BOOK

Hooray for Amanda & Her Alligator!
By Mo Willems. Illus. by the author. HarperCollins/Balzer + Bray, 2011. 72p. Ages 4–8
The theme of "surprise" runs through this collection of short friendship stories. Playful humor and relationship dynamics are on typically spot-on display here as Amanda and her toy alligator surprise one another; one time with a new, third friend. Characteristic clean cartoon-style illustrations on a white background keep the action front and center.

Ling & Ting: Not Exactly the Same!
By Grace Lin. Illus. by the author. Little, Brown, 2010. 48p. (DC) Ages 5–8
Six short easy-to-read stories feature twins Ling and Ting, who might look the same but are different in many ways. The girls get their hair cut (an overzealous snip caused by a sneeze makes it easier to tell them apart),

make dumplings, practice magic tricks, and more. Colorful, flat oil and pastel illustrations complement the simple, repetitive text; the friendship and fun these Chinese American sisters share ring true. GEISEL HONOR BOOK

Nursery Rhyme Comics: 50 Timeless Rhymes from 50 Celebrated Cartoonists

By Leonard S. Marcus (ed.). Illus. by various artists. First Second, 2011. 128p. Ages 3-8

Give fifty comics creators a nursery rhyme each and what do you get? An incredibly upbeat modern take on classic childhood ditties. The artists represented differ wildly in style, from Mike Mignola's dark retelling of "Solomon Grundy" to Kate Beaton's whimsical "Duke of York," but they all share an earnestness and joy in their presentation of these one- to three-page rhymes. While the rhymes themselves are fine for young children, the book resonates most with more experienced readers who are familiar with the rhymes and can embrace the humor found in the illustrations.

Penny and Her Doll

By Kevin Henkes. Illus. by the author. Greenwillow, 2012. 32p. Ages 4-7

Mouse girl Penny and her mother are in the garden when the mailman arrives with a package from her grandmother: a new doll. As Penny's mother and father take care of her siblings, they try to offer her suggestions for naming it, but nothing feels right, until Penny stops thinking so hard about it and just lets the name come to her. Penny's voice is authentic, and her play and interaction with her doll will be recognizable to children. The interaction between Penny and her family, conveyed through resonant prose and watercolor-and-ink scenes, rings true. The sight words and repetition are just right for emerging readers, here and in *Penny and Her Song* (2012).

Penny and Her Song

By Kevin Henkes. Illus. by the author. Greenwillow, 2012. 32p. Ages 4-7

With her verve and good cheer, a mouse named Penny is an easy character to like, and young readers will enjoy getting to know her better through this new series including *Penny and Her Doll* (2012). Here, Penny is just bursting to share the new song she has learned at school with her family. But everyone is just too busy and it's just not the right time. Penny impatiently waits her turn, but it's worth the delay as Mama and Papa join in—even donning costumes—as her twin younger siblings are lulled into sleep.

Rabbit & Robot: The Sleepover

By Cece Bell. Illus. by the author. Candlewick, 2012. 56p. Ages 5-7

Rabbit's carefully planned sleepover for his friend Robot goes awry when he discovers that Robot's idea of a good time is very different from his own. For example, Robot prefers nuts, bolts, and screws to pizza, which he procures by taking apart Rabbit's furniture. The humorous easy-reading text is accompanied by goofy cartoon illustrations. This is a good choice for readers who are ready to transition from easy readers to more advanced texts. GEISEL HONOR BOOK

Zig and Wikki in the Cow

By Nadja Spielgelman. Illus. by Trade Loeffler. TOON, 2012. 40p. Ages 5-8

In their second adventure, the two aliens named Zig and Wikki lose their spaceship on Earth and, as they try to find it, nearly lose their friendship as well. While they're friends, the two have distinct personalities, and major problems like losing their spaceship highlight their differences. To get their spaceship back, Zig and Wikki actually have to travel through a cow, learning about ecology—and cow dung—in the process. This deft mix of scientific fact, humor, and grossness is enhanced by cartoon illustrations that underline the comedic outrageousness of the story. Their first adventure is chronicled in *Zig and Wikki in Something Ate My Homework* (2010).

Chapter Books

Recommendations for cultivating a diverse collection are indicated by "(DC)."

The Adventures of Nanny Piggins

By R. A. Spratt. Illus. by Dan Santat. Little, Brown, 2010. 256p. Ages 9-11

Memorable nannies are prevalent in children's novels, but Nanny Piggins is exceptional. The porcine wonder arrives at the door of the Green family as though she were shot from a cannon. Considering that was her former occupation, it is the first of many surprises for Derrick, Samantha, and Michael as they adjust to the unpredictable ways of their unapologetic and plucky caregiver. Eating chocolate for every meal, adopting a dancing Russian bear, and sailing the high seas are just a few of the escapades experienced under the care of the one and only Nanny Piggins, whose story is continued in *Nanny Piggins and the Wicked Plan* (2012).

Big Nate: In a Class By Himself
(Big Nate series)

By Lincoln Peirce. Illus. by the author. HarperCollins, 2010. 224p. Ages 8-12

A winning combination of text, comics, and humor introduce a larger-than-life character in this first Big Nate book. Big Nate's day begins like any other—avoiding his annoyingly perfect big sister and trying to swallow his dad's lumpy oatmeal. On his way to school Nate discovers a fortune cookie proclaiming, "Today you will surpass all others," a prediction he believes will prove his greatness to teachers and classmates alike. Through doodles, sidebars, and mini comics, readers discover that all Big Nate is destined for is detention. Nate subsequently finds his stride in *Big Nate On a Roll* (2011).

Captain Underpants: Captain Underpants and the Terrifying Return of Tippy Tinkletrousers
(Captain Underpants series)

By Dav Pilkey. Illus. by the author. Scholastic, 2012. 304p. Ages 7–10

This hilariously antic prelude to the popular series returns to the kindergarten days of his two main characters, George Beard and Harold Hutchins, showing how they first bonded in their efforts to defeat the school's sixth-grade bully, Kipper Krupp. The familiar kid-friendly blend of illustrations and text tells how young George and Harold—who aren't yet gifted with superpowers—instead use their wits to try to destroy the power Kipper holds over the other students.

Clara Lee and the Apple Pie Dream

By Jenny Han. Illus. by Julia Kuo. Little, Brown, 2011. 160p. Ages 6–9

Third grader Clara Lee loves talk to friends and read but doesn't like multiplication. She loves her Korean-born Grandpa, who lives with her family in the United States and tells her that a bad dream is a sign of good fortune. Clara Lee wants to be named Little Miss Apple Pie in her town's annual Apple Blossom Celebration, but to earn that title she has to speak at an all-school assembly. Will her speech be better than a fifth grader's? This family-and-friendship story is spiced with humor and drama.

Clementine: Clementine, Friend of the Week
(Clementine series)

By Sara Pennypacker. Illus. by Marla Frazee. Disney/Hyperion, 2010. 176p. Ages 7–10

Clementine, a spirited third grader, is chosen to be "Friend of the Week," an honor that allows her to be the line leader, collect the milk money, and share her autobiography with the entire class. The best part is the booklet she is given in which her classmates share their kind words and other compliments. However, over the course of the week, she gets into a fight with her best friend and her pet cat goes missing. Clementine must learn how to still be a good friend even while overcoming her own set of problems.

Clementine: Clementine and the Family Meeting
(Clementine series)
By Sara Pennypacker. Illus. by Marla Frazee. Disney/Hyperion, 2011. 160p. Ages 7-10

Clementine is worried about the meaning of a family meeting, but it turns out to not be necessarily bad news, although Clementine isn't happy about it: a new baby is coming. Meanwhile, she's working on a science project with a friend and their rat subject disappears. This early chapter book is just right for the middle-grade audience; the humor isn't overdone and is leavened with real heart.

Dyamonde Daniel Books: Almost Zero
(Dyamonde Daniel Books series)
By Nikki Grimes. Illus. by R. Gregory Christie. Putnam, 2010. 128p. (DC) Ages 8-10

In this third installment in the Dyamonde Daniel series, Dyamonde wants a pair of red high-top sneakers like the ones her stylish classmate Tameka is wearing. Dyamonde tells her mother that it is her job as a mother to give her what she needs, but her mother provides her with only what she needs and "nothing more." When her classmate loses everything she owns in a fire, Dyamonde is motivated to help and learns a significant life lesson. The black-and-white ink drawings and accessible text are engaging and entertaining; fans can find more in *Halfway to Perfect* (2012), listed in the next entry.

Dyamonde Daniel Books: Halfway to Perfect
(Dyamonde Daniel Books series)
By Nikki Grimes. Illus. by R. Gregory Christie. Putnam, 2012. 96p. (DC) Ages 8-10

The fourth entry in the Dyamonde Daniel series takes on a serious issue: tween concern about weight. Dyamonde knows Damaris doesn't need to lose weight, but the comments the girls hear from their peers make it easy to seem like it's impossible to be too thin. The message here has the potential to be didactic and heavy handed, but the realistic dialogue and situations keep the friendship story accessible.

Ellie McDoodle: Best Friends Fur-Ever
(Ellie McDoodle series)

By Ruth McNally Barshaw. Illus. by the author. Bloomsbury, 2010. 176p. Ages 8-12

Ellie "McDoodle"—so nicknamed for her drawing ability—is thrilled when she's asked to pet-sit Alix, an African grey parrot. It's perfect timing since Ellie plans to do her school assignment on grey parrots and hopes to train Alix to recite it for her. But Ellie's life gets complicated when Alix flies out the front door. Ellie is an engagingly imperfect heroine whose woes will resonate with young readers. Other pluses include the mix of text and illustrations, a plethora of jokes, and instructions on how to play a related game and make a leopard puppet. Fans can follow Ellie's further adventures in *Ellie McDoodle: Most Valuable Player* (2012).

Ellie McDoodle: Most Valuable Player
(Ellie McDoodle series)

By Ruth McNally Barshaw. Illus. by the author. Bloomsbury, 2012. 176p. Ages 8-12

It's not easy for a normally unathletic kid to join the soccer team, and matters only get more complicated when it turns out Ellie's dad will be the coach. Ellie will have to make a choice of which competition to participate in when the soccer tournament and the Journey of the Mind (an academic club) tournament occur on the same day. Kids learning to discern for themselves which after-school activities are the most important to them will recognize Ellie's angst.

J. J. Tully Mystery: The Trouble with Chickens
(J. J. Tully Mystery series)

By Doreen Cronin. Illus. by Kevin Cornell. HarperCollins/Balzer + Bray, 2011. 128p. Ages 8-10

J. J. is a retired hero. After seven years of being a search-and-rescue dog who has tracked the six-day-old scent of a lost hiker and been flown first-class to France to find a skier lost in the Alps, he is presented with a different challenge: find mama hen's two lost chicks. Each chapter in this well-paced mystery reveals new clues mingled with snappy one-liners. Spoiler alert: the obnoxiously adorable chicks steal the show. This is a humorous first book in the J. J. Tully Mystery series with satisfying plot twists and a smart detective; he's in action again in *The Legend of Diamond Lil* (2012).

Knights' Tales: The Adventures of Sir Balin the Ill-Fated
(Knights' Tales series)

By Gerald Morris. Illus. by Aaron Renier. Houghton Mifflin Harcourt, 2012. 128p. Ages 8-11

The Knights' Tales series brings medieval characters to life for contemporary kids, using humor alongside traditional folkloric aspects of the Knights' exploits. In the fourth installment, Sir Balin learns not to put too much stock in prophecies as he goes about the knightly business of questing and the like. Black-and-white line art adds a comedic element and helps break up the text, making these accessible entries to the grand tradition of heraldic literature. The feats of an even more famous knight are recounted in *The Adventures of Sir Gawain the True* (2011), listed next.

Knights' Tales: The Adventures of Sir Gawain the True
(Knights' Tales series)

By Gerald Morris. Illus. by Aaron Renier. Houghton Mifflin Harcourt, 2011. 128p. Ages 8-11

The exploits of one of the greatest knights of King Arthur's Round Table come to life in a rousing and often comical chapter book. A brave and accomplished fighter, Sir Gawain falls short in the areas of courtesy. A tricky challenge from the magical Green Knight puts the hero's life in mortal peril, but he continues through lively adventures involving a mysterious dwarf, an unconquered swordsman, and other colorful characters. The irreverent narrative is peppered with humor and occasionally silliness but also explores ideas of chivalry and friendship in thought provoking ways. Further adventures are heralded in *The Adventures of Sir Balin the Ill-Fated* (2012).

Liberty Porter, First Daughter: Cleared for Takeoff
(Liberty Porter, First Daughter series)

By Julia DeVillers. Illus. by Paige Pooler. Simon & Schuster/Aladdin, 2012. 224p. (DC) Ages 8-11

Bits of trivia about United States presidents and the White House are couched in this readable story about what life as a White House kid might be like, such as the fact that every President except George Washington has lived there, the fact that more than one million tourists visit there every year, and more. Liberty's everygirl voice and wry humor make her relatable, even if her adventures aren't something everyday kids do. This time, she's off to Tblisi, Georgia, with her parents on a diplomatic mission.

Liberty Porter, First Daughter: Liberty Porter, First Daughter
(Liberty Porter, First Daughter series)

By Julia DeVillers. Illus. by Paige Pooler. Simon & Schuster/Aladdin, 2010. 192p. (DC)
Ages 8-11

This timely series stars Liberty Porter, the daughter of the recently elected President of the United States, who is African American. With the real-life election of the first African American president, more kids than even can envision themselves living in the White House, and it's fun to conjecture about just how realistic this portrayal might be.

Liberty Porter, First Daughter: New Girl in Town
(Liberty Porter, First Daughter series)

By Julia DeVillers. Illus. by Paige Pooler. Simon & Schuster/Aladdin, 2010. 208p. (DC)
Ages 8-11

In this second entry in the Liberty Porter: First Daughter series, Liberty has just moved to Washington, DC, and must deal with the same kinds of issues all new kids do, especially how to make new friends. Actual facts about living in the White House and black-and-white spot illustrations add interest; fans can follow Liberty's story in *Cleared for Takeoff* (2012).

Lulu and the Brontosaurus

By Judith Viorst. Illus. by Lane Smith. Simon & Schuster/Atheneum, 2010. 128p. Ages 6-10

Lulu, a demanding, spoiled child, wants a brontosaurus as a pet for her birthday. When her parents refuse the request, she runs away to find one herself, only to find the tables turned when she finds a brontosaurus who wants Lulu as *his* pet. This creative treatment occasionally breaks the "fourth wall" between writer and reader and offers three possible endings.

Origami Yoda: Darth Paper Strikes Back
(Origami Yoda series)

By Tom Angleberger. Illus. by the author. Abrams/Amulet, 2011. 176p. Ages 9-11

In this hilarious sequel to *The Strange Case of Origami Yoda* (2010), Harvey's dark side, Darth Paper, is introduced. Out of spite, Harvey sets Dwight up as the number one troublemaker at Ralph McQuarrie Middle School. Tommy tries to save Dwight from expulsion by compiling another case file, with chapter titles such as "Origami Yoda and the Pre-eaten

Wiener" and "Origami Yoda and the Exploding Pizza Bagels" to prove Dwight's unconventional but positive contributions in front of the school board. The treatment of middle school concerns and relationships rings true here, couched with humor and kindness. Fans won't want to miss the follow-up *The Secret of the Fortune Wookiee* (2012).

Origami Yoda: The Secret of the Fortune Wookiee
(Origami Yoda series)
By Tom Angleberger. Illus. by the author. Abrams/Amulet, 2012. 208p. Ages 9-11

Trouble ensues when Dwight, the student whose Origami Yoda finger puppet seemingly solved many kids' personal problems, is suspended from McQuarrie Middle School. Suddenly, students who have relied on Origami Yoda's sage advice are forced to cope without him. Fortunately it seems that Dwight has provided an Origami Yoda substitute: it's a Chewbacca finger puppet, which the middle schoolers immediately dub a "Fortune Wookiee." Yet it's just not the same, and Dwight's friends, appalled to learn that he's lost his motivation to return to McQuarrie, work to persuade him that he—and Origami Yoda—are irreplaceable. Backstory can be found in *The Strange Case of Origami Yoda* (2010) and *Darth Paper Strikes Back* (2011).

Origami Yoda: The Strange Case of Origami Yoda
(Origami Yoda series)
By Tom Angleberger. Illus. by the author. Abrams/Amulet, 2010. 160p. Ages 9-11

When the kids at McQuarrie Middle School need advice, many turn to Origami Yoda. His advice may sound strange ("All of pants you must wet!"), but somehow it always works out. Is Origami Yoda a true source of deep wisdom? Or is he really just a paper puppet on the finger of a weird sixth grader? This story unfolds through the pages of a case file filled with funny cartoons and multiple viewpoints from a believable cast of kids. Humor is the main appeal, but it's balanced by gentle insights into middle school social dynamics, continued in *Darth Paper Strikes Back* (2011) and *The Secret of the Fortune Wookiee* (2012).

Stink: Solar System Superhero
By Megan McDonald. Illus. by Peter H. Reynolds. Candlewick, 2010. 128p. Ages 5-8

Stink is, as he says, "cuckoo for Pluto." So Stink is devastated when he learns that a group of scientists have decided that Pluto no longer qualifies as a planet. And it's particularly bad since Stink's second-grade archenemy Riley Rottenberger is happy about Pluto's demotion. But Stink's second-grade teacher comes up with a way to resolve the question (and inject some learning) by challenging Stink and Riley to a Pluto debate. This story brims with both facts and fun, highlighted by light-hearted drawings scattered throughout.

Sugar Plum Ballerinas: Dancing Diva
(Sugar Plum Ballerinas series)

By Whoopi Goldberg and Deborah Underwood. Illus. by Maryn Roos. Disney/Jump at the Sun, 2012. 160p. (DC) Ages 7–10

Sometimes being chosen to play the lead isn't enough for a true diva. In this case, Epatha thinks she can improve on the choreography with her own ideas and the other Sugar Plums try to bring her down to earth.

Sugar Plum Ballerinas: Perfectly Prima
(Sugar Plum Ballerinas series)

By Whoopi Goldberg and Deborah Underwood. Illus. by Maryn Roos. Disney/Jump at the Sun, 2010. 160p. (DC) Ages 7–10

This celebrity-authored series looks light and fluffy, and maybe it is. But it also addresses themes that will ring true to young girls with a realistic cast of multicultural characters. This time, Jerzey aspires to become a ballerina, but she doesn't seem to have the natural talent to achieve her ambitious goals. Things get worse before they get better (but eventually they do improve) when her embarrassing little brother visits ballet class. Subsequent entries include *Terrible Terrel* (2010), *Sugar Plums to the Rescue!* (2011), and *Dancing Diva* (2012).

Sugar Plum Ballerinas: Sugar Plums to the Rescue!
(Sugar Plum Ballerinas series)

By Whoopi Goldberg and Deborah Underwood. Illus. by Maryn Roos. Disney/Jump at the Sun, 2011. 160p. (DC) Ages 7–10

A couple of high-interest topics intersect in this installment of the Sugar Plum Ballerinas series: ballet and kittens. When Jessica finds a stray kitten to rescue, she hopes it can stay at the Nutcracker School of Ballet until there is room at the animal shelter. Unfortunately, the school itself has lost its lease, and its demise may be hastened if the landlord finds out there is an animal living there. The Sugar Plums come together to solve yet another problem.

Sugar Plum Ballerinas: Terrible Terrel
(Sugar Plum Ballerinas series)

By Whoopi Goldberg and Deborah Underwood. Illus. by Maryn Roos. Disney/Jump at the Sun, 2010. 160p. (DC) Ages 7–10

Terrel isn't so terrible; she just wants (and expects) to have her own way most of the time since she's the one who keeps her brothers (and sometimes her single father) in line. She is in for a surprise, though, when her father brings a new girlfriend on a father-daughter outing. That's not the worst, though—it turns out the girlfriend's niece is Terrel's competitor for queen bee of the ballet studio.

Super Diaper Baby 2: The Invasion of the Potty Snatchers

By Dav Pilkey. Illus. by the author. Scholastic/Blue Sky, 2011. 192p. Ages 6–8

With its potty humor and deliberate grammatical errors and misspellings, this second book starring Super Diaper Baby isn't likely to be a first choice with parents. But grownups can't deny the kid appeal of the comic format and madcap action featuring Super Diaper Baby and Diaper Dog battling Dr. Dinkle, a.k.a. Rip Van Tinkle, and his evil-sidekick cat, Petey. Yes, the book's black-and-white illustrations look primitive, and the plot is definitely puerile. But that will be just fine with young readers, including reluctant ones.

Young Fredle

By Cynthia Voigt. Illus. by Louise Yates. Knopf, 2011. 224p. Ages 8–12

Fredle is a young, curious mouse who resides with his family in a comfy nest hidden behind the pantry wall. One day, he is kicked out after getting sick from gorging on candy. Without the shelter of the pantry, he is soon discovered by the homeowners and transplanted outside. Once in the outer world, Fredle wrestles with homesickness and loneliness but soon meets new creatures and discovers other ways of living. Along his journey, Fredle finds excitement and beauty as he explores the definition of home.

Novels

Recommendations for cultivating a diverse collection are indicated by "(DC)."

90 Miles to Havana

By Enrique Flores-Galbis. Roaring Brook, 2010. 304p. (DC) Ages 9-12

In 1960s-era Havana, Cuba, Julian and his family flee their homeland for freedom as their country is transformed during the Cuban Revolution. Julian and his brothers are sent ahead to Miami, Florida, as part of the Pedro Pan Operation; there, they endure hardships that are emotional and physical as they cope with separation from their parents and homeland.
BELPRÉ HONOR BOOK FOR NARRATIVE

As Easy as Falling Off the Face of the Earth

By Lynne Rae Perkins. Greenwillow, 2010. 352p. Ages 12-14

On his way to summer camp, fifteen-year-old Ry discovers that the program has been canceled. When he gets off the train to call his grandfather, it leaves without him, and he's stranded in the middle of nowhere. Meanwhile, his grandfather falls down and hits his head, resulting in amnesia; his parents are unreachable on a sailboat in the Caribbean. Sure, it's implausible, but the journey really is the destination as Ry and his new friend Del try to get Ry back to his home and family.

The Batboy

By Mike Lupica. Philomel, 2010. 256p. Ages 10-14

Brian Dudley is due for a win, and finally, he might have a chance. He hasn't had much of a winning streak, especially since he lost his dad to baseball. Cole Dudley decided a while ago the game was more import-ant than family and moved across the world to coach. But this summer will be different. Brian's lined up a dream job: batboy for his town's major league team. When his hero returns to the team, Brian must step up to the plate and accept that heroes—and dream jobs—aren't always what we hope them to be.

Beauty Queens

By Libba Bray. Scholastic, 2011. 400p. Ages 12-14

In this slightly futuristic, sardonic fun-house mirror of a media-crazed society, a group of teen beauty pageant contestants find themselves crash landed on a (supposedly) deserted island. They must use their wits, the salvaged beauty products, and leadership skills in order to survive. Unbe-known to these beauty queens, the Corporation manipulates everyone's moves, and an evil foreign dictator plots world domination on the island. Readers soon discover that the first impression of each young woman defi-nitely does not tell the whole story, and a cast of unconventional beauty queens, including a transgendered teen, will provoke much thought on the priorities in current culture.

Between Shades of Gray

By Ruta Sepetys. Philomel, 2011. 352p. Ages 12-14

In 1941 Lithuania, fifteen-year-old Lina creates beautiful artwork and wishes for a future of romance and happiness. Her dreams are bru-tally shattered when her family is torn apart and transported to Siberia by Soviet officers under the order of Stalin as part of a massive race-cleansing scheme. Separated from her father, Lina, her mother, and her brother labor in Siberia under subhuman conditions along with millions of other deportees, digging for beets and fighting for survival. Through-out this cruel experience, Lina and her family maintain dignity and hope in this compelling story based on historical facts.

Beyonders: A World without Heroes
(Beyonders series)
By Brandon Mull. Simon & Schuster/Aladdin, 2011. 464p. Ages 10-13

Jason's life is boring, and he's tired of it. However, getting transported from the hippo enclosure at the zoo, to an unknown and unstable land, is not what he was expecting when he looked for excitement. Jason finds himself in the land of Lyrian, a dangerous place ruled by the evil emperor Maldor. There are no resistors left, having all been defeated, and the people are desperate for a hero. In this fast paced, exciting start to a new series, Jason and his new companion Rachel must learn to be the heroes Lyrian desperately needs. The series continues with *Seeds of Rebellion* (2012).

Beyonders: Seeds of Rebellion
(Beyonders series)
By Brandon Mull. Simon & Schuster/Aladdin, 2012. 512p. Ages 10-13

This action-packed second installment in the Beyonders trilogy continues Jason and Rachel's adventures from *A World Without Heroes* (2011) in their efforts to help Prince Galloran defeat evil Maldor, but they are beset by powerful foes and the possibility of a spy in their midst.

Bitterblue
By Kristin Cashore. Illus. by Ian Schoenherr. Dial, 2012. 576p. Ages 13-14

In this companion novel to *Graceling* (2009) and *Fire* (2009), it has been eight years since the killing of Leck, the King of Monsea, who had been a violent psychopath with mind-controlling abilities. After his death, his young daughter Bitterblue was made Queen. Now eighteen, Bitterblue is struggling to come to terms with the monstrous legacy of her father. Suspecting that her advisors are not telling her the truth about conditions in her kingdom, Bitterblue disguises herself as a commoner and sneaks out at night to attempt to discover the truth about her father's reign and heal the still-festering wounds he has created. With the help of friends, Bitterblue uncovers a dangerous web of secrets that cause her to reevaluate everything she has been told and whom she can trust.

Bluefish
By Pat Schmatz. Candlewick, 2011. 240p. Ages 10-14

When Travis and his alcoholic grandfather move, he must find new ways to hide old secrets. His new friend Velveeta seems determined to uncover them, despite desperately hiding her own. Travis is intrigued by her feisty attitude; she seems so full of life, when he feels so empty, especially after his beloved dog, Rosco, goes missing. With depth and honesty, this novel explores the meaning of friendship and family and how to overcome making mistakes.

Books of Beginning: The Emerald Atlas
(Books of Beginning series)

By John Stephens. Illus. by Grady McFerrin. Knopf, 2011. 432p. Ages 9-12

Ten years ago on Christmas Eve, the parents of Kate, Michael, and Emma mysteriously disappeared. In the years to follow, the three children make the rounds among several orphanages before landing at the mansion of an eccentric doctor. While there, the curious trio uncovers a magic atlas that transports them fifteen years into the past where they meet a younger version of their caretaker as well as other fantastical beings, some good, some evil. This adventure blends fantasy with kid dialogue that rings true and wraps up in a satisfying but not-too-neat way. Those hungry for more can follow this up with *The Fire Chronicle* (2012).

Books of Beginning: The Fire Chronicle
(Books of Beginning series)

By John Stephens. Illus. by Grady McFerrin. Knopf, 2012. 400p. Ages 9-12

Time travel marks this follow-up to *The Emerald Atlas* (2011), in which Kate finds herself in New York one hundred years earlier while Michael and Emma try to find the second Book of Beginning. Fans of the earlier volume will welcome this one, and a brief summary allows entry to the series at this point as well.

Breaking Stalin's Nose

By Eugene Yelchin. Illus. by the author. Holt, 2011. 160p. Ages 10-13

Ten-year-old Sasha Zaichik's life takes a dramatic turn overnight when his father, a Communist officer in the Soviet Union, is arrested. He starts to act up, breaking a classmate's eyeglasses with a snowball and damaging a statue of his idol, Comrade Stalin. The first-person narration brings the Cold War–era Russian setting to life for contemporary kids as Sasha must cope with the dissolution of his aspiration to become a Soviet Young Pioneer and meet Comrade Stalin. NEWBERY HONOR BOOK

The Candymakers

By Wendy Mass. Illus. by Steve Scott. Little, Brown, 2010. 464p. Ages 9–12

Each of the four twelve-year-old contestants in a candy-making competition tells their sides of a complex mystery where the readers are kept guessing all the way to the end. Young readers will find the unique motivations and perspectives of each character intriguing and discover, along with the narrators, the true meaning of friendship and the dangers of presumptions in this delicious treat of a tale.

Charlie Joe Jackson: Charlie Joe Jackson's Guide to Extra Credit
(Charlie Joe Jackson series)

By Tommy Greenwald. Illus. by J. P. Coovert. Roaring Brook, 2012. 272p. Ages 9–12

This follow-up to *Charlie Joe Jackson's Guide to Not Reading* (2011) stars the middle schooler in his attempt to avoid being sent to a dreaded reading-themed summer camp by amassing extracurricular extra credit. Slackers and readers alike will relate to this realistic take on middle school life, even beyond academics to the dynamics of which-girls-like-which-boys and vice versa.

Charlie Joe Jackson: Charlie Joe Jackson's Guide to Not Reading
(Charlie Joe Jackson series)

By Tommy Greenwald. Illus. by J. P. Coovert. Roaring Brook, 2011. 224p. Ages 9–12

A well-liked middle school kid with nice friends and family, Charlie Joe Jackson doesn't have much to complain about and he knows it. In this first book in the series, Charlie Joe is determined to never read a book and will go to extraordinary lengths to ensure it. This first-person account captures what kids really think about their reading assignments in short chapters interspersed with entertaining nonreading tips. Charlie Joe's complicated schemes to avoid reading and his strategic but flawed advice will hook reluctant—and enthusiastic—readers right away. Cartoon-like illustrations suit the pithy narrative, which is continued in *Charlie Joe Jackson's Guide to Extra Credit* (2012).

The Cheshire Cheese Cat: A Dickens of a Tale

By Carmen Agra Deedy and Randall Wright. Illus. by Barry Moser. Peachtree, 2011. 228p. Ages 8-12

Charles Dickens, his writings, and other nineteenth-century literary allusions play a part in this story about Skilley, the new mouser at Ye Olde Cheshire Cheese Inn. Skilley loves cheese but he does not eat mice! In fact, he loves cheese so much that he agrees to protect the inn's mice if they will provide him with the inn's delicious cheese. There are a number of characters, such as Maldwyn, Her Majesty's Raven, and the evil cat, Pinch, who complicate the arrangement and add mystery and danger to this delightful animal fantasy.

Chickadee

By Louise Erdrich. Illus. by the author. HarperCollins, 2012. 208p. (DC) Ages 10-12

In the fourth installment of the Birchbark House saga, eight-year-old Chickadee is kidnapped, escapes his captors, and encounters people of European descent for the first time. Some mean well, some do not. Fans of the prior books in the series will recognize the lyrical writing and focus on quotidian details that bring life to the larger themes.

Chronicles of Egg: Deadweather and Sunrise
(Chronicles of Egg series)

By Geoff Rodkey. Illus. by Iacopo Bruno. Putnam, 2012. 304p. Ages 10-14

In this swashbuckling adventure of pirates and hidden treasure, a young boy finds himself suddenly orphaned and somehow must figure out which direction to turn and whom to trust in his overturned world. Delightfully quirky, the narrative in this new series bursts with descriptions that evoke the heat and stink of Deadweather and the pleasant, cool breezes of Sunrise. There is unexpected depth to this fantasy-adventure, as "Egg" begins to understand that things are not always what they seem and learns to trust his own judgment.

Cinder

By Marissa Meyer. Feiwel & Friends, 2012. 400p. Ages 12-14

Cinder makes her home on a future planet Earth, where war and disease has ravaged the population. She has survived a terrible fire that left her not only an orphan but a cyborg: less than human, an outcast of society. She is unloved by her adoptive stepmother and is forced to work to support her family. But as a cyborg, she has special skills with machines, and when the Prince comes looking for New Beijing's best mechanic, pieces of the classic Cinderella story fall into place in this refreshing take on an old tale.

Clockwork Angel
By Cassandra Clare. Simon & Schuster/Margaret K. McElderry, 2010. 496p. Ages 12-14

Sixteen-year-old Tessa Gray stumbles upon the Downworld in Gothic Victorian London and is surprised to find herself part of the elaborate battle scheme between Shadowhunters and Demons. The angelic Shadowhunters, with their special weapons, are guardians against Demons and Vampires who prey on humans. Tessa must decide on her next moves that will affect not only the fate of her beloved brother and her new found love, but also the fate of all mankind in this entertaining concoction of Angels, Demons, and Vampires spiced with torturous romance, gore, and inventive automatons.

Cosmic
By Frank Cottrell Boyce. HarperCollins/Walden Pond, 2010. 320p. Ages 9-12

Liam's above-average height is the frequent cause for mistakes about his age and abilities. As a preteen with early hair growth, Liam is taken for an adult in several situations. While his parents fret over the implications, Liam rolls with the misassumptions most of the time, especially when allowed on height-requirement thrill rides. When Liam wins a contest through his father's cell phone provider, his identity and existence are taken to a whole new level as he accepts a free trip to space. This tall tale is rooted in the humorous dreams and realities of a twelve-year-old British boy.

Countdown
By Deborah Wiles. Scholastic, 2010. 400p. Ages 11-14

During the time of Cuban Missile Crisis, eleven-year-old Franny, daughter of an F-1 pilot, finds her own personal universe deteriorating. The sudden betrayal by a best friend, the secret messages her activist older sister receives and hides, and the embarrassment of an elderly uncle whose obsession with building a bomb shelter have turned the family into the neighborhood's laughingstock. The historical backdrop of Franny's tale of growth and revelation is furthered enhanced by the thoughtfully and effectively selected images, quotes, and biographical sketches of important social figures of the time.

Daughter of Smoke and Bone

By Laini Taylor. Little, Brown, 2011. 420p. Ages 12-14

Seventeen-year-old art student Karou leads a double life: she's an art student by day, but at night she enters a magical doorway to work for her surrogate father, a "chimaera" wish monger. Karou seldom questions her role or her origins until she meets and falls in love with the dangerously alluring Akiva, an avenging "seraphim," whose mission is to murder all chimaeras. Reminiscent of the story of Romeo and Juliet, this dark fantasy romance keeps the tension, and interest, high.

The Dead

By Charlie Higson. Disney/Hyperion, 2011. 480p. Ages 11-14

In this gripping prequel to the popular postzombie-apocalyptic *The Enemy* (2009), a global viral outbreak turns all people above age sixteen into flesh-eating creatures. The young students at the Rowhurst boarding school find themselves hunted by teachers and infected teens. Fighting their way out of the woods, they met Greg, an adult who claims to be immune to the disease and offers to help them by driving them to safety on a school bus. Their journey to survival is perilous and full of treachery, gore, and high-octane action sequences.

Diary of a Wimpy Kid: Cabin Fever
(Diary of a Wimpy Kid series)

By Jeff Kinney. Illus. by the author. Abrams/Amulet, 2011. 224p. Ages 9-12

All kids get cabin fever in the winter, and Greg Heffley is no exception. Especially during the seemingly endless month between Thanksgiving and Christmas, it's hard to keep a lid on tween energy, and these diary entries prove it. Once again, deceptively simple line drawings express perfectly the everykid emotions represented in this first-person account.

Diary of a Wimpy Kid: The Third Wheel
(Diary of a Wimpy Kid series)

By Jeff Kinney. Illus. by the author. Abrams/Amulet, 2012. 224p. Ages 9-12

The diary format continues to work well for fans of the Diary of a Wimpy Kid series, making Greg Heffley's quotidian adventures immediate and real for young readers. This time, Greg's approaching the cusp of his teenage years and experiencing all the angst that goes along with that milestone, including perhaps a change of best friends, girls, acne, and parental attempts at helping with homework.

Diary of a Wimpy Kid: The Ugly Truth
(Diary of a Wimpy Kid series)

By Jeff Kinney. Illus. by the author. Abrams/Amulet, 2010. 224p. Ages 9-12

The fifth book in this super popular series features tween challenges of not being a kid anymore, but not yet a real grown-up, and trying to make new friends after parting with some of the old ones. The trademark wry humor and realistic situations will ring true for tweens; as always, the line art (think *Harold and the Purple Crayon* for older kids) breaks up the text, making it more accessible. Greg's quotidian adventures continue in *Cabin Fever* (2011) and *The Third Wheel* (2012).

Don't Call Me Hero

By Ray Villarreal. Arte Público/Piñata, 2011. 208p. (DC) Ages 12-14

Latino everykid Rawly Sanchez is dealing with a lot of issues: he's flunking algebra; his dad has died of lung cancer, even though he never smoked; and Rawly wishes he could be a hero instead. His wish comes true when he unselfishly saves a girl from a prominent wealthy family from a fatal car crash. Rawly's newfound status brings its own challenges, and tweens will eagerly read along as he tackles them.

The Dreamer

By Pam Muñoz Ryan. Illus. by Peter Sís. Scholastic, 2010. 372p. (DC) Ages 10-14

Rich with magical images, this poignant account of Chilean poet Pablo Neruda's childhood reveals his pain and isolation growing up with a controlling father and also foreshadows the poet's future writing voice. Even though the story revolves around Neruda's dysfunctional family, this is not a story of abuse and recovery but rather a moving celebration of the strength and resilience of the creative spirit. The magical realism in the text is perfectly complemented by imaginative illustrations; both text and art are faithful to the spirit of Neruda's poetry. BELPRÉ AWARD FOR NARRATIVE

The Extraordinary Mark Twain (According to Susy)

By Barbara Kerley. Illus. by Edwin Fotheringham. Scholastic, 2010. 48p. Ages 7-11

Mark Twain perhaps had no better biographer than his eldest daughter Susy. In the spring of 1885, teenage Susy began recording her candid observations of her father in a journal that she hid under her pillow. She affectionately and honestly described both his flaws and virtues, which are quoted throughout this book, complete with misspellings. Author Barbara Kerley supplements her research with Susy's unique perspective to showcase Twain's complex personality as a "funny, serious, absentmined, cat-loving, billiard-playing, philosophical Papa."

Fake Mustache: How Jodie O'Rodeo and Her Wonder Horse (and Some Nerdy Kid) Saved the U.S. Presidential Election from a Mad Genius Criminal Mastermind

By Tom Angleberger. Illus. by Jen Wang. Abrams/Amulet, 2012. 208p. Ages 9-11

The Heidelberg Handlebar Number Seven, made with real human hair, gives its wearer supreme hypnotizing powers. Twelve-year-old Casper obtains this fake mustache to carry out his outlandish world-dominating plans: from robbing the Hairsprinkle Federal Gold Reserve by sending a gang of school librarians with ninja moves to rigging the upcoming presidential election. His best friend Lenny bravely goes after Casper to thwart his evil schemes with the help of TV's teen celebrity, Jodie O'Rodeo, and some inventive gadgets such as chicken-tasting erasers and a "sticky stretchy rubber" hand.

Falling In

By Frances O'Roark Dowell. Simon & Schuster/Atheneum, 2010. 272p. Ages 9-12

A door in the principal's office leads Isabelle Bean into a strange world where children wander the woods to avoid a witch who eats babies. Or so they say. The curiosity and imagination that made Isabelle an outcast at school serve her well in this adventure, as she learns the truth about the witch, discovers a secret about herself, and makes some true friends for the first time ever. A playful narrative voice that frequently addresses the reader provides comic relief amid the suspense and surprises of the tale.

The False Prince

By Jennifer A. Neilsen. Scholastic, 2012. 352p. Ages 10-12

Sage, a fourteen-year-old orphan and a cunning thief, is captured by the king's regent, along with two other orphan boys. All three are trained in court politics, geography, sword fight, and other necessary skills to impersonate the long lost Prince Jaron in a treasonous plot. However, only one shall succeed; the two who fail will undoubtedly be disposed of. Sage's snappy, rebellious, and highly unreliable first-person narrative often conceals key pieces of information and thus heightens the tension of this entertaining and action-packed novel of truths and lies, alliances and betrayals, and false steps and triumphs.

The Familiars

By Adam Jay Epstein and Andrew Jacobson. HarperCollins, 2010. 368p. Ages 8-12

While being chased by a ferocious shadowhound, Aldwyn, a streetwise alley cat, ducks into a pet shop to hide. However, this is a store of extraordinary creatures known as familiars, "animal companions of wizards and witches." Once bonded, familiars share their unique magical talents with their human. Mistaken for being a familiar, Aldwyn is chosen by Jack, a young wizard-in-training. When Jack, his sister, and his best friend are all captured by an evil queen, Aldwyn must join forces with two other familiars, a chatty tree frog and a snobbish blue jay, in order to rescue their "loyals."

The Girl Who Circumnavigated Fairyland in a Ship of Her Own Making

By Catherynne M. Valente. Illus. by Ana Juan. Feiwel & Friends, 2011. 256p. Ages 10-14

Once upon a time, September "grew very tired indeed of her parents' house," and longed for an adventure. So when she is invited to Fairyland by a Green Wind and a Leopard, she accepts. However, Fairyland is not what September has imagined. Stalked by an evil marquess, September must work with her new friends—a book-loving dragon and a boy named Saturday who is almost human—to restore order and revive Fairyland. This eloquent saga, first published in installments on the Internet, is filled with intriguing characters and beautiful language and will be read again and again.

The Grand Plan to Fix Everything

By Uma Krishnaswami. Illus. by Abigail Halpin. Simon & Schuster/Atheneum, 2011. 266p. (DC) Ages 9–12

Best friends Dini and Maddie enjoy Bollywood films starring Dolly Singh and are dismayed when Dolly announces her retirement. When Dini's family moves to India for two years, the girls connect with e-mails, letters, and phone calls. Dini also reaches out to Dolly Singh, encouraging her to resume acting, and is convinced that if only she could find Dolly and talk to her in person she could persuade her to make more movies. The girls' friendship rings true in any culture, and details of life in India and Indian culture add interest.

Griffin & Co. Adventures: Framed
(Griffin & Co. Adventures series)

By Gordon Korman. Scholastic, 2010. 240p. Ages 9–11

An outlandish plot that unfolds via realistic tween dialogue and characters that ring true are hallmarks of this series starting Griffin, "The Man with the Plan," and his friend Savannah and her Great Dane. This time, Griffin ends up in the JFK (jail for kids) Alternative Education Center, under a charge of stealing a former student's Super Bowl ring, and he and his band of wannabe detectives have to find the real culprit. This fun detective series includes *Showoff* (2012) as well as previous titles *Swindle* (2008) and *Zoobreak* (2009).

Griffin & Co. Adventures: Showoff
(Griffin & Co. Adventures series)

By Gordon Korman. Scholastic, 2012. 256p. Ages 9–11

Griffin Bing, the "Man with the Plan," is back, and this time he needs to rescue giant Doberman Luthor from the pound and turn him into a show dog, after Luthor accidentally causes a stage to collapse at a dog show. As in other series entries, the plot adroitly combines hilarity and mystery; sure, it's implausible, but tons of fun for animal lovers and mystery fans alike.

Heart of a Samurai

By Margi Preus. Abrams, 2010. 320p. (DC) Ages 10–14

Based on true events, this historical novel tells the story of fourteen-year-old Manjiro, who is rescued in 1841 by an American whaling ship after a shipwreck leaves him and his companions stranded on a remote island. Eventually, the ship's captain adopts Manjiro and takes him to his home in Massachusetts. Manjiro, the first known Japanese person to come to the United States, learns English and American customs, as well as how to cope with racial prejudice. Manjiro bridges two worlds, and after returning to Japan ten years later, works to persuade the Japanese Shogun to end Japan's isolationist policy and to foster communication between Japan and the United States.

Heroes of Olympus: The Lost Hero
(Heroes of Olympus series)
By Rick Riordan. Disney/Hyperion, 2010. 560p. Ages 10-13

Riordan returns to Camp Half-Blood with another high-velocity series, Heroes of Olympus. Although Percy Jackson from *The Lightning Thief* (2005) is still a part of this Camp Half-Blood world, this new installment is centered on three teenagers, Jason, Piper, and Leo. Told in the third person, each chapter focuses on one of these three characters. This time the characters are older, so there is a bit more teenage angst. This is Riordan's storytelling at its best: familiar Greek and Roman mythology, a prophecy to unravel, a quest to fulfill, clever plot twists, and witty banter. The saga continues in *The Son of Neptune* (2011) and *The Mark of Athena* (2012).

Heroes of Olympus: The Mark of Athena
(Heroes of Olympus series)
By Rick Riordan. Disney/Hyperion, 2012. 600p. Ages 10-13

In this third action-packed installment of the Heroes of Olympus series, following *The Lost Hero* (2011) and *The Son of Neptune* (2011), Percy is reunited with Annabeth. The top young heroes of Camp Jupiter and Camp Half-Blood join forces to face a series of highly demanding and dangerous quests. On board the airship Argo, traveling through the United States and finally landing in Rome, they exorcise the Eidolons (spirits that possess people and machines), escape from the deathtrap housed inside Georgia Aquarium, defeat the twin giants Ephialtes and his brother Otis, and most importantly, find and close The Doors of Death.

Heroes of Olympus: The Son of Neptune
(Heroes of Olympus series)

By Rick Riordan. Disney/Hyperion, 2011. 544p. Ages 10-13

After waking up from a strange, long sleep, Percy Jackson finds himself at the Roman demigod training camp with most of his memory gone. This time, he embarks on a perilous quest to free Thanatos, the god of Death, imprisoned in Alaska. Accompanied by two new heroes, Hazel from New Orleans, who has the gift of gathering treasures from the earth, and Frank, the part-Chinese son of Mars, who can shapeshift, Percy encounters the befuddled but infinitely informative book-devouring harpy Ella, the powerful Amazons who run the online megastore, and an army of giants. This follows Percy's adventures in *The Lost Hero* (2011) and precedes them in *The Son of Neptune* (2012).

Hidden

By Helen Frost. Farrar/Frances Foster, 2011. 160p. Ages 11-14

In a gripping opening sequence, eight-year-old Wren hides in a stolen car for several days before escaping. Only the thief's daughter, a girl named Darra, knew she was there. Six years later, the girls unexpectedly reunite at a summer camp. Their reactions to this meeting, along with their memories of the traumatic event, come alive through evocative poetry: Wren's words are free verse, while Darra's are rendered in an invented two-layered form. The dynamic poetry captures the highly charged emotions of two characters who share vivid memories of an experience that both would rather forget.

Hurricane Dancers: The First Caribbean Pirate Shipwreck

By Margarita Engle. Holt, 2011. 160p. (DC) Ages 12-14

This historical novel in verse tells the story of Quebrado, the son of a Taíno mother and a Spanish father, who has been captured as a slave by pirates. When a hurricane destroys the ship, Quebrado is able to escape but cannot run forever from his past. Narration from alternating perspectives and a vibrant portrayal of the Caribbean setting bring history to life for contemporary readers. BELPRÉ HONOR BOOK FOR NARRATIVE

Inheritance
(Inheritance Cycle series)

By Christopher Paolini. Random, 2011. 860p. Ages 12-14

In this concluding volume in the wildly popular Inheritance Cycle, Eragon assumes a leadership role in accomplishing many tasks: discovering and protecting the unhatched dragon eggs; defeating, with the help of former villain Murtagh, the tyrant king Galbatorix; and uniting warring groups to create a peaceful world where dragons can be bonded to not just humans and elves but dwarves and Urgals as well. Despite the presence of a few hints about future stories from Alagaësia, this is an eventful and satisfying ending to Eragon's long quest to restore the glorious legacy of the Dragon Riders.

Inside Out and Back Again

By Thanhha Lai. HarperCollins, 2011. 272p. (DC) Ages 10-14

Forced by the fall of Saigon in 1973 to leave a happy life in Vietnam, young Hà flees with her family to the United States, where she struggles to adjust to a new country. Addressing difficult issues of war, loss, and prejudice, the emotion of this historical novel is lightened by Hà's humor and strength. Contemporary American kids will relate to the universal emotions and fears expressed here, even as they learn about another culture, where a favorite treat is toasted coconut eaten at the street market. NEWBERY HONOR BOOK

Junonia

By Kevin Henkes. Greenwillow, 2011. 192p. Ages 8-12

This poignant coming-of-age novel is titled after a type of seashell. Alice Rice visits Sanibel Island, Florida, with her family every year in February. This year at the beach is special, however, because Alice, an only child, is turning ten. She has grown up surrounded by adults her whole life and begins to explore the tension between being a child and becoming a young adult herself, symbolized by her search for the rare junonia shell.

Kane Chronicles: The Red Pyramid
(Kane Chronicles series)

By Rick Riordan. Disney/Hyperion, 2010. 528p. Ages 10-13

Since their mother's death six years ago, twelve-year-old Sadie Kane has lived in London with her maternal grandparents while her older brother, fourteen-year-old Carter, has traveled the world with their father, Dr. Julius Kane, an African American Egyptologist. When Carter and Sadie accompany their father to the British Museum, Dr. Kane accidentally unleashes five Egyptian gods, including the villainous god Set. After their father disappears, Carter and Sadie embark on a dangerous journey to save him, discover that they possess magical powers, and learn about their family's lineage that goes back to the time of the pharaohs. Told in the alternating voices of Carter and Sadie, this riveting story cleverly incorporates Egyptian history, mythology, and archaeology. More adventures of the Kane family are featured in *The Throne of Fire* (2011) and the conclusion, *The Serpent's Shadow* (2012).

Kane Chronicles: The Serpent's Shadow
(Kane Chronicles series)

By Rick Riordan. Disney/Hyperion, 2012. 406p. Ages 10-13

The struggle against Egyptian serpent god Apophis that began in *The Throne of Fire* (2011) continues, as Sadie and Carter Kane battle him with help from fellow magicians and other Egyptian gods; the goal this time is not just to defeat Apophis, but destroy him. In this affecting conclusion to the Kane Chronicles series, the teenagers merge themselves with Egyptian gods so their powers can be enhanced sufficiently to prevail.

Kane Chronicles: The Throne of Fire
(Kane Chronicles series)

By Rick Riordan. Disney/Hyperion, 2011. 464p. Ages 10-13

Carter and Sadie Kane's magical powers are growing in strength, and as fans of the first episode in the Kane Chronicles, *The Red Pyramid* (2010), will expect, the siblings are not afraid to use magic in sometimes unorthodox (technically illegal?) ways. In this episode of the Kane Chronicles, Carter and Sadie must stop an evil magician from unleashing the Egyptian serpent god Apophis to wreak havoc on the world. Action-packed, suspenseful pacing keeps readers riveted.

Keeper

By Kathi Appelt. Illus. by August Hall. Simon & Schuster/Atheneum, 2010. 416p. Ages 10-13

Ten-year-old Keeper has had the worst day ever and she is unintentionally responsible for it. Her guilt and disappointment impel her to take off in a small boat into the Gulf of Mexico with her dog, BD, in search of her long-lost mother, Meggie Marie. Keeper believes that Meggie Marie is a mermaid who swam away when Keeper was three, and if she can find her, everything will be fixed. Rhythmic descriptions veering from the realistic to the mystical aptly capture the feeling of Keeper's journey of longing and self-discovery.

Legend

By Marie Lu. Putnam, 2011. 320p. Ages 11-14

This dystopian novel is set in the "Republic," formerly the western United States. When infamous fifteen-year-old Day, on the government's most-wanted list for murdering a security officer, is pitted against June, a prodigy soldier in the most prestigious training school, the action heats up. In alternating chapters told in the two main characters' voices, June soon discovers that her views on the Republic and Day may not be completely accurate, and Day finds himself attracted to his assassin, realizing that she might be his best asset in his desperate effort to save his family.

Liar & Spy

By Rebecca Stead. Random/Wendy Lamb, 2012. 208p. Ages 9-12

There are two mysteries intertwined in this story about new neighbors Georges's and Safer's burgeoning friendship: one of the conventional type (is a murderer living in their building?), the other a more sad, personal one involving Georges's mother and just why she spends so much time at the hospital, even more than a nurse pulling double shifts normally would. Sadness is leavened with humor and realistically portrayed characters; the hopeful ending satisfies without making any unrealistic promises.

Liesl & Po

By Lauren Oliver. Illus. by Kei Acedera. HarperCollins, 2011. 320p. Ages 9-13

A young girl lives locked in an attic, a lonely orphan runs errands for an angry alchemist, two ghosts shift from the Other Side, and these seemingly disparate stories eventually weave together to create an overarching fantastical mystery. Liesl is a girl and Po is a ghost, but that doesn't stop them from working together to put her deceased father's ashes to rest and learn to cope with loss and move on.

Long Lankin

By Lindsey Barraclough. Candlewick, 2012. 464p. Ages 12-14

Based on an old English ballad, this is a bone-chilling tale of ancient evil and secrets long-buried. When Cora and her little sister are sent away from London to stay with a great-aunt, they become entangled in a horrifying mystery that surrounds the village of Bryers Guerdon. The first-person narration switches smoothly between main characters and time periods as the mystery gradually unwinds.

A Long Walk to Water: Based on a True Story

By Linda Sue Park. Clarion, 2010. 128p. (DC) Ages 11-13

This eloquent novel, written in dual-narrative, tells of the intertwined lives of two young people growing up in Sudan decades apart. Nya lives in Southern Sudan in 2008; every day she must collect water for her family, an eight-hour ordeal. She walks to and from the pond, carrying the jug by herself. Salva's story begins in Southern Sudan in 1985 during the Second Sudanese Civil War. Fleeing for his life, Salva walks to safety over many miles and years. Based on a true story, this deftly captures the life-changing journeys of Nya and Salva.

Maximilian & the Mystery of the Guardian Angel: A Bilingual Lucha Libre Thriller

By Xavier Garza. Illus. by the author. Cinco Puntos, 2011. 160p. (DC) Ages 8-12

A fast-paced plot, likeable characters, bilingual text, and some spot cartoon-style art to break up the text make this mystery especially accessible and fun. Here, eleven-year-old Maximilian dreams of becoming a *lucha libre* wrestler and must try to foil the villains who are trying to defeat his wrestling hero, *El Angel de la Guarda*. BELPRÉ HONOR BOOK FOR NARRATIVE

The Mighty Miss Malone

By Christopher Paul Curtis. Random/Wendy Lamb, 2012. 320p. (DC) Ages 9-12

Twelve-year-old Deza Malone is a charming and exceptionally smart student on the right track. However, in 1936 Gary, Indiana, the Great Depression is in full swing, and her family's situation is deteriorating: Deza's teeth are rotting, her brother is not growing at a normal rate, and Mrs. Malone is thinner than ever. Her father leaves in pursuit of steady work in Michigan, promising to send for them; as time goes on and he does not, the family goes in search of him and ends up living in a Hooverville outside of Flint. The narrative, from the point of view of Deza, the "Mighty Miss Malone," displays humor and warmth and brings this historical period to life for contemporary kids.

Mockingbird

By Kathryn Erskine. Philomel, 2010. 240p. Ages 9-13

Written in the voice of ten-year-old Caitlin, this is an emotional and honest glimpse into a young person's struggle to adapt to a violently changed world. Caitlin must deal with a violent shooting in her community—one that took her older brother's life. But dealing with it is even more challenging for Caitlin, who has Asperger's Syndrome. How do you talk it out when you don't like to talk at all? How Caitlin learns to cope makes for a powerful and unforgettable story, written as a response to the 2007 Virginia Tech shootings.

Mockingjay

By Suzanne Collins. Scholastic, 2010. 400p. Ages 11-14

In this powerful conclusion to the Hunger Games trilogy, Katniss is used as an effective pawn for the revolution. She appears in propaganda films staged to incite discontent and muster the courage of the oppressed districts. Although the cause seems noble, Katniss disagrees with the way the leaders of the revolution manipulate the public and must make difficult choices that will determine the fate of the entire nation. Although the trilogy ends with disturbing events showing the ill effects of war for all involved, the somber epilogue still lends a ray of hope.

A Monster Calls

By Patrick Ness. Illus. by Jim Kay. Candlewick, 2011. 224p. Ages 10-14

It is 12:07 a.m. and a monster has come calling for Conor. But it is not the monster he was expecting, the one from his nightmare. Why is this monster here for him, and why does it insist that it was Conor himself who called it? It claims to be seeking the very thing Conor is most afraid of: the truth. Haunting and powerful, this novel explores themes of fear and shame and death and loss with depth and compassion. Stark illustrations bring the monster to life.

Moon Over Manifest

By Clare Vanderpool. Delacorte, 2010. 368p. Ages 9-13

The Great Depression has its grip on 1936 Manifest, Missouri, where twelve-year-old Abilene Tucker is sent to live after having spent most of her childhood riding the rails with her father. It's a more stable existence, but not completely placid: Abilene learns more about her father and why he originally left Manifest and uncovers a local mystery in the process. The narrative is an appealingly complex blend of first-person voice, newspaper columns, and archival letters from a World War I soldier. NEWBERY MEDAL

The Mostly True Story of Jack

By Kelly Barnhill. Little, Brown, 2011. 323p. Ages 8-12

Jack is abruptly dumped off at his kooky aunt and uncle's house for what he expects to be a long, boring summer. When he gets there, he finds some new friends who seem a little wacky too, each having had a strange and ominous premonition prior to his arrival. The mysteries of the town and what's going on there, including what seem to be powerful dark forces, unravel bit by bit, making connections among people and the natural world that keep readers riveted.

My Life as a Stuntboy

By Janet Tashjian. Illus. by Jake Tashjian. Holt/Christy Ottaviano, 2011. 272p. Ages 9-12

Reluctant reader Derek Fallon is back in the second book in the My Life as a . . . series, which began with *My Life as a Book* (2010). This time twelve-year-old Derek has the opportunity to be a stunt double in a film and as a result learns some lessons about friendship and trust. Here again, the humorous middle school environment rings true with authentic, albeit sometimes annoying, characters in abnormal situations. The spot-on snarky attitude in the text is complemented by amusing stick-figure drawings illustrating challenging words.

My Sister Lives on the Mantelpiece

By Annabel Pitcher. Little, Brown, 2012. 224p. Ages 12-14

Ten-year-old Jamie doesn't remember his sister and doesn't miss her the way the rest of the family does. Is something wrong with him somehow? And how can Rose, who has been dead for five years, still manage to tear his family apart? Things are about to get even worse: his new friend is

Muslim, and Jamie's dad says that Muslims killed his sister. Equally heart-wrenching and laugh-out-loud funny, this is a memorable tale of friendship and reconciliation that deals with timely issues.

Ninth Ward

By Jewell Parker Rhodes. Little, Brown, 2010. 224p. (DC) Ages 9-12

Mama Ya-Ya has raised Lanesha since she was born, and the two share a special gift of "sight." When Hurricane Katrina approaches New Orleans, Mama Ya-Ya "sees" a danger coming beyond the actual storm but doesn't know what it is. She becomes ill and must rely on Lanesha to prepare. As the levees break and the waters rise, Lanesha looks toward her mother's spirit for guidance. Readers experience the disaster from Lanesha's perspective as she struggles to survive along with her friend TaShon. CORETTA SCOTT KING AUTHOR HONOR BOOK

Okay for Now

By Gary D. Schmidt. Clarion, 2011. 368p. Ages 10-14

This companion to the Newbery Honor Book *The Wednesday Wars* (2007) set in the late 1960s features Doug Swieteck, who's frustrated after his father is fired and the family moves to a tiny town where Doug has trouble making friends. How is he to make it through the day with an angry father, a new house people call "The Dump," and a brother coming home with war wounds? A sarcastic girl, a baseball hero, Doug's interest in Audubon's bird portraits, and more combine to create a story with honesty and heart.

On the Day I Died

By Candace Fleming. Random/Schwartz & Wade, 2012. 208p. Ages 12-14

Snippets of Chicago history and actual facts about real places are embedded in this collection of eerie ghost stories, all set in the Windy City. Teen Mike Kowalski enters a Chicago cemetery one night and meets a series of teenaged ghosts, each of whom tells the story of how he or she died. Al Capone, the cemetery (which is a real cemetery in Chicago today), a now closed insane asylum, and more feature in these creepy tales.

The One and Only Ivan

By Katherine Applegate. Illus. by Patricia Castelao. HarperCollins, 2012. 320p. Ages 8-12

Narration by a gorilla is fairly unusual in children's literature, but here, Ivan articulates what it's like to live in cage from an animal's perspective;

this time, in a rundown roadside attraction along with Stella, an aging elephant. The animals cope by making friends with one another, a stray dog, and the custodian's daughter, who seems to understand them better than most humans do. When a baby elephant is brought in to revive the fading appeal of the Big Top Mall and Video Arcade, Ivan knows he has to act to help her avoid his and Stella's fate. NEWBERY MEDAL

One Crazy Summer

By Rita Williams-Garcia. HarperCollins/Amistad, 2010. 224p. (DC) Ages 9-11

Three sisters, Delphine, Vonetta, and Fern, travel to Oakland, California, in the summer of 1968 to visit their mother who abandoned them seven years ago. When they arrive, the mother makes them buy and eat Chinese dinners, tells them not to go into the kitchen, and sends them to the summer camp sponsored by the Black Panthers. The education Delphine, Vonetta, and Fern receive from both the Black Panthers and their mom makes for a memorable summer the girls will never forget. CORETTA SCOTT KING AUTHOR AWARD

Out of My Mind

By Sharon Draper. Simon & Schuster/Atheneum, 2010. 304p. (DC) Ages 10-13

Melody, an eleven-year-old girl born with cerebral palsy, is unable to speak, walk, or control her muscles, and her ability to move is severely limited. Because of this, most people assume that she is mentally impaired and does not have the ability to learn. Yet Melody's condition affects her body but not her mind; she is highly intelligent and has a photographic memory. Melody's life changes when inclusion classrooms are introduced in her school and she interacts with children other than those in her special needs class. When Melody receives "Elvira," her Medi-Talker computer that allows her to communicate with others, her classmates and teachers begin to realize how much she has to offer. She and her classmates must learn how to interact when she becomes part of the debate team and travels to competitions with her "typical" peers.

Peter Nimble and His Fantastic Eyes

By Jonathan Auxier. Illus. by the author. Abrams/Amulet, 2011. 400p. Ages 9-12

Conventional wisdom here is that blind children make the best thieves: they have an incredible sense of smell, and their little fingers can slip through the tiniest keyhole. And Peter is the best of these thieves; that is, until he steals a box containing three sets of wonderful, magical eyes. As he tries on the first pair, he is immediately transported to a strange and hidden island and tasked with rescuing a lost kingdom. Peter must rely on some odd and unlikely friends to complete his quest. This fantastical adventure story addresses compelling themes of destiny and friendship.

Popularity Papers: Research for the Social Improvement and General Betterment of Lydia Goldblatt & Julie Graham-Chang
(Popularity Papers series)

By Amy Ignatow. Illus. by the author. Abrams/Amulet, 2010. 208p. (DC) Ages 9-12

At the start of the Popularity Papers series, fifth graders and lifelong friends Lydia and Julie undertake a study of just what makes girls "popular." The results, written in notebook format, ring true for those on the cusp of tweenhood. Weightier issues are alluded to as well; for example, Julie lives with her two dads. Refreshingly, this isn't the focus but is treated as an everyday fact; the heart of the story remains the two girls and their friendship.

Popularity Papers: The Long-Distance Dispatch between Lydia Goldblatt & Julie Graham-Chang
(Popularity Papers series)

By Amy Ignatow. Illus. by the author. Abrams/Amulet, 2011. 208p. (DC) Ages 9-12

Lifelong friends Lydia and Julie correspond with e-mail and sketch letters after Lydia moves to London with her family. They share the ups and downs of making friends in new junior high schools: Julie enters the popular clique while Lydia cajoles a group she names the Outcasts into joining the drama club. Their drawings and comments reveal social observations and increasing self-realization with abundant humor and just enough emotional drama. Lydia's single mom and Julie's two dads are models of contemporary earnest, loving parents. This sequel to *Research for the Social Improvement and General Betterment of Lydia Goldblatt & Julie Graham-Chang* (2010) can also stand alone; further adventures are chronicled in *Words of (Questionable) Wisdom from Lydia Goldblatt and Julie Graham-Chang* (2011) and *The Rocky Road Trip of Lydia Goldblatt & Julie Graham-Chang* (2012).

Popularity Papers: The Rocky Road Trip of Lydia Goldblatt & Julie Graham-Chang
(Popularity Papers series)

By Amy Ignatow. Illus. by the author. Abrams/Amulet, 2012. 208p. (DC) Ages 9-12

This time, Lydia's and Julie's adventures take place over the summer, rather than in school, when they take a road trip with Julie's two dads at the wheel. This amount of time together reveals new insights about friendships and family relationships, even as the girls continue their quest to figure out the secret of popularity.

Popularity Papers: Words of (Questionable) Wisdom from Lydia Goldblatt and Julie Graham-Chang
(Popularity Papers series)

By Amy Ignatow. Illus. by the author. Abrams/Amulet, 2011. 208p. (DC) Ages 9-12

Lydia and Julie are nearing the end of sixth grade, and they are beginning to deal with some more grown-up issues, such as the death of another friend's mother. Along the way, their daily reciprocal journal entries continue to reveal realistic, appealing tween dialogue and situations.

Ranger's Apprentice: Erak's Ransom
(Ranger's Apprentice series)

By John Flanagan. Philomel, 2010. 384p. Ages 10-13

The seventh series entry returns to an earlier point in the story arc, just before Will finishes his apprenticeship and becomes a full ranger himself. Here, Will and his friends must journey to the desert to free their friend Erak. The nonstop action and compelling characters fans of the series have come to expect are on display again and will leave readers more than ready for the next adventures in *The Kings of Clonmel* (2010), *Halt's Peril* (2010), *The Emperor of Nihon-Ja* (2011), and *The Lost Stories* (2011).

Ranger's Apprentice: Halt's Peril
(Ranger's Apprentice series)

By John Flanagan. Philomel, 2010. 320p. Ages 10-13

Halt the Ranger, his apprentice Will, and Horace are on the trail of some outlaws when Halt is injured by an outlaw arrow and the two boys must take over. Elements that characterize the appeal of earlier books in the series are on display here again: just enough menace to keep up suspense, coupled with victorious teamwork and a satisfying conclusion that still leaves room for more.

Ranger's Apprentice: The Emperor of Nihon-Ja
(Ranger's Apprentice series)

By John Flanagan. Philomel, 2011. 352p. Ages 10-13

Although this is the close of the popular Ranger's Apprentice series, it's not too late to introduce a new element: a new culture, the empire of Nihon-Ja, which seems to be loosely based on Japan. Halt, Will, and the others aren't simply going to go off into the sunset; there is one last major battle to win, this time against a band of samurai who wish to unseat the Emperor.

Ranger's Apprentice: The Kings of Clonmel
(Ranger's Apprentice series)

By John Flanagan. Philomel, 2010. 368p. Ages 10-13

Fans of the series who are curious about Halt's background will be pleased with the eighth title in the Ranger's Apprentice series, where much of his backstory is revealed when he, Will, and Horace visit Clonmel. The immediate action concerns a plot by a religious cult that Halt, Will, and Horace seek to defeat; the intertwining of episodic events within the larger story arc is particularly satisfying in this volume.

Ranger's Apprentice: The Lost Stories
(Ranger's Apprentice series)

By John Flanagan. Philomel, 2011. 352p. Ages 10-13

Just as it seemed to be over, here are some "director's cuts": adventures of the main characters in the Ranger's Apprentice series that didn't make it into the original nine books. These stories include more about Horace, Will's family background, and how Halt first became a Ranger. Inspired by questions from real-life readers, this is an extremely satisfying finishing touch.

The Ring of Solomon

By Jonathan Stroud. Disney/Hyperion, 2010. 416p. Ages 10-13

The cantankerous djinni, Bartimaeus of Uruk, is back in a prequel to the popular Bartimaeus Trilogy. While the setting for the trilogy is modern London, The Ring of Solomon, a stand-alone novel, takes place in

950 BCE Jerusalem where King Solomon the Great of Israel rules, wearing a ring of immense power. Bartimaeus gets into one uproarious adventure after another. The setting for this historical fantasy is a believable backdrop for the various magicians and spirits. Bartimaeus is a fully realized character with surprising depth and unsurpassed wit; he literally steals every scene and captures the heart of every reader.

The Scorpio Races

By Maggie Steifvater. Scholastic, 2011. 416p. Ages 13-14

Inspired by Manx, Irish, and Scottish legends of beautiful but deadly water horses that emerge from the sea, this tale of fantasy, romance, and adventure is set on the island of Thisby, where the *capaill uisce*, or water horses, emerge each autumn. Carnivorous and predatory, they endanger the islanders and are much faster than regular horses. Once a year, the water horses are raced on the beach, and the competition is often fatal to the riders. The narrative alternates between the first-person voices of seasoned champion Sean Kendrick and Kate "Puck" Connolly, a hopeful newcomer, who gradually develop a friendship and budding romance.

Scumble

By Ingrid Law. Illus. by Brandon Dorman. Dial, 2010. 416p. Ages 10-13

There's a reason Ledger's family is so unusual: When they turn thirteen, their "savvy" makes its appearance. The savvy, a magical talent, can be a gift or a curse. Unfortunately for Ledger, his savvy is especially chaos inducing; it literally dismantles all man-made constructions without Ledger even touching them. This companion novel to *Savvy* (2008), offers another gentle coming-of-age yarn with the tone of a tall tale. Ledger's plight will tug at heartstrings and tickle funny bones as he learns about himself and to value his unique ability.

Secret: This Isn't What It Looks Like
(Secret series)

By Pseudonymous Bosch. Illus. by Gilbert Ford. Little, Brown, 2010. 432p. Ages 8-12

Max-Ernest is desperate. His best friend Cass, a fellow member of the secret Terces Society, is in a coma, and he has to help find a cure to awaken her. But Max-Ernest also has to contend with increasingly violent efforts by the evil Midnight Sun group to keep Terces Society members from learning the all-important Secret. This fourth volume in the popular "Secret" series by the mysterious and aptly named Pseudonymus Bosch contains the same heady mix of silliness, adventure, and magic—combined with a dash of second-person narration—that have proved such a hit with readers. Volume five continues the action with *You Have to Stop This* (2011).

Secret: You Have to Stop This
(Secret series)
By Pseudonymous Bosch. Illus. by. Gilbert Ford. Little, Brown, 2011. 384p. Ages 8-12

The final entry in the Secret series poses some new questions before answering the most pressing mysteries in a satisfying ending that isn't too neat. The setting this time is a natural history museum, where the accidental breaking of an ancient mummy's finger sets the plot into action. As in previous books, the mystery and suspense is leavened with wry humor, including some breaking of the "fourth wall" between author and reader.

Secrets at Sea
By Richard Peck. Illus. by Kelly Murphy. Dial, 2011. 272p. Ages 9-11

When the Cranston family sails to England to find their daughter a husband, the Cranston mouse family follows despite their fear of water. Fanciful black-and-white spot illustrations highlight the shipboard adventures, and the first-person account told from the point of view of Helena, the oldest mouse sibling, appeals.

Ship Breaker
By Paolo Bacigalupi. Little, Brown, 2010. 336p. Ages 11-14

In a destroyed but recognizable future, young Nailer suffers a cruel and meager life working on a salvage team near a flooded New Orleans. Survival depends on how fast he and his crew work, but working too fast can cost them their lives. When a clipper ship is wrecked in a fierce storm, Nailer must choose between rich salvage and the life of the shipwreck's lone survivor. A stark, haunting setting and characters that explode from the page draw readers into the depths of this savage world.

Sidekicks
By Jack D. Ferraiolo. Abrams/Amulet, 2011. 320p. Ages 10-14

For Scott Hutchinson, it isn't easy being an anonymous prep school student by day and a superhero sidekick by night. Scott, also known as Bright Boy, is an accomplice to Phantom Justice, the alias of Scott's crime-fighting guardian, Trent Clancy. Modern superheroes (and supervillains) can either be gifted with superstrength, superspeed, or superintelligence. While Bright Boy and Phantom Justice are strong and agile, their nemesis is reputed for his notorious scheming. When this villain breaks out of prison and reunites with this own sidekick, Monkeywrench, Scott must help put an end to their evil plans.

So For Real: Cool like That
(So For Real series)

By Nikki Carter. Kensington/Dafina, 2010. 240p. (DC) Ages 13-14

In the fourth installment in the So For Real series, Gia Stokes and her best friend Ricky are going to New York City to attend a summer enrichment program. Gia and Ricky like each other but have not made their relationship official, and Gia hopes Ricky will make his move while they are together in New York. Along comes Rashad, an irresistible cutie who is also in the summer enrichment program. He is definitely making some moves on Gia. What will Ricky do? What will Gia do?

Son

By Lois Lowry. Houghton Mifflin Harcourt, 2012. 400p. Ages 12-14

This long-awaited conclusion to the Giver quartet, focuses on fourteen-year-old Claire, who had given birth to Gabriel, the baby Jonas rescued in *The Giver* (1993). Immediately after he's born, Claire's son is taken to the communal nursery. Breaking the rules, she visits him regularly until Jonas disappears with him. Claire sets out to find him and ends up in an isolated village, suffering from amnesia. Her attempts to regain her memory and find her son eventually lead her to Gabriel, Jonas, and Kira, from *The Giver*, *Gathering Blue* (2000), and *Messenger* (2004). Although Claire's story stands alone, it will be of highest interest to fans of the others.

Starry River of the Sky

By Grace Lin. Illus. by the author. Little, Brown, 2012. 288p. (DC) Ages 8-11

Rooted in elements of Chinese folklore, as was *Where the Mountain Meets the Moon* (2009), this elegantly told original tale brings together a series of seemingly unconnected stories to wind up neatly at the end, as interconnected parts of the same puzzle. Here, Rendi has run away from home and ends up working in an inn where he's compelled to tell one story of his own for every one that a storytelling guest named Madame

Chang relates; together the stories answer the mystery of what has happened to the moon.

A Tale Dark and Grimm

By Adam Gidwitz. Illus. by Hugh D'Andrade. Dutton, 2010. 256p. Ages 9-12

Within the first few pages, readers are warned that this book is not for the faint of heart. Scheming witches, dark warlocks, and vengeful hunters lurk within this gruesome retelling of the Grimms' fairy tales, beginning with the bloody origins of Hansel and Gretel and how they were born to murderous parents. Then the twins are cast as heroes in a series of other, equally harrowing Grimm tales, retold here with a dark sense of humor. Jack and Jill wend their way through more similarly grim tales in *In a Glass Grimmly* (2012).

Three Times Lucky

By Sheila Turnage. Dial, 2012. 320p. Ages 9-14

A set of interlocking mysteries characterizes this gripping read set in a rural North Carolina town. Where did Miss Moses LaBeau, or "Mo," come from before she was rescued as an infant from a basket floating in a stream? What is the true identity of her amnesiac adoptive father? And is there a murderer on the loose? NEWBERY HONOR BOOK

Trash

By Andy Mulligan. Random/David Fickling, 2010. 240p. Ages 12-14

Three "dumpsite boys" find a valuable leather bag among the mountains of trash that serves as their home. Rather than turn it in for a reward, the kids decide to unravel the mystery of the bag's origins. As they stay just one step ahead of police, the boys enter unfamiliar worlds of power, wealth, and corruption. Strong characters, expert plotting, and a richly textured, slightly futuristic urban setting make this a novel that's both thrilling and thought provoking. The moral courage and the eventual triumph of three kids with all odds against them are especially satisfying.

The Trouble with May Amelia

By Jennifer L. Holm. Illus. by Adam Gustavson. Simon & Schuster/Atheneum, 2011. 224p. Ages 9-12

This sequel to the Newbery Honor Book *Our Only May Amelia* (1999) focuses on a difficult year for May Amelia's family in rural Washington

State in 1900. May Amelia is thirteen and must cope with a family in which she doesn't seem to belong and the heavy responsibility of helping her Finnish-speaking father negotiate a land deal that goes bad. The not-too-neat ending reflects the reality of the time period, which makes sense since some plot elements are based on the author's own family history.

Turtle in Paradise

By Jennifer L. Holm. Random House, 2010. 208p. Ages 8-12

Eleven-year-old Turtle doesn't think 1935 Key West, Florida, is paradise at all after she is abruptly sent there to live with relatives while her mother works in New Jersey. She finds coping with the change difficult, but things get more interesting when she discovers a buried treasure map. NEWBERY HONOR BOOK

The Underdogs

By Mike Lupica. Philomel, 2011. 256p. Ages 9-13

Twelve-year-old Will Tyler is fast, talented, and loves to play football. When his cash-strapped town cancels the football season, he secures funding and builds a team determined to beat their well-funded rival. Football enthusiasts will appreciate the play-by-play descriptions and plays including "Go-7-Go" and "34 Counter." Satisfying subplots infused with humor depict multifaceted players and parents overcoming conflicts and personal challenges, including learning to play well with Hannah Grayson, the first girl in town to play on a boys' team.

Ungifted

By Gordon Korman. HarperCollins/Balzer + Bray, 2012. 288p. Ages 10-13

An unfortunate collision involving a bronze statue and large glass doors turns out to be one prank too many for troublemaker Donovan Curtis. Fortunately, a computer mix-up results in his immediate transfer to a new school: an academy for gifted students, where he plans to lay low and stay out of trouble. But how can an average student with a penchant for mischief fit in with a bunch of scholastically brilliant and socially clueless geniuses? Crisp dialogue and engaging characters provide plenty of humor, along with sharp insights about the true natures of intelligence, popularity, and friendship.

Warriors: Omen of the Stars: Night Whispers
(Warriors: Omen of the Stars series)

By Erin Hunter. HarperCollins, 2010. 352p. Ages 10-13

This installment of the Warriors: Omen of the Stars series offers descriptions of cat communication, claw to jaw combat, sibling rivalry, light romance, herbal healing, and characters who question truth, loyalty, and justice. Thunder Clan members grapple with the scope and value of their special powers and struggle to carry out orders received from their mystical communications with Star Clan ancestors to end sharing between clans and adopt a code of each clan for itself. As a result, border clashes and violence intensify as the clans prepare for a brutal battle with the Dark Forest. Reading the series in sequence is recommended; next up is *Sign of the Moon* (2011).

Warriors: Omen of the Stars: Sign of the Moon
(Warriors: Omen of the Stars series)

By Erin Hunter. HarperCollins, 2011. 352p. Ages 10-13

The fourth title in the series seems designed to set up future action; here, the four clans of cats are experiencing heightened tension, and there are hints that some sort of secret prophecy may hold the answer to how any battle among them will sort out.

We Could Be Brothers

By Derrick D. Barnes. Scholastic, 2010. 176p. (DC) Ages 10-13

Robeson Battlefield and Pacino Clapton have very different lives. Robeson comes from a financially stable family that emphasizes learning and achievement. Pacino comes from a rough neighborhood with a different emphasis. However, they have something in common, a boy name Tariq who is the reason Robeson and Pacino have postschool suspension. Can Robeson and Pacino accept their differences and become friends in order to face their common enemy.

Western Mysteries: The Case of the Deadly Desperados
(Western Mysteries series)

By Caroline Lawrence. Putnam, 2012. 272p. Ages 10-14

Twelve-year-old P. K. Pinkerton is in a tight spot when he returns home to find his adoptive parents murdered and himself now the target of an outlaw known as "Whittlin' Walt" and his gang. There's quite a bit to this historical mystery (the launch of a new series) set in 1862, including some features of the main character—half Sioux and half of European descent—that contemporary readers might recognize as signs of Asperger's Syndrome.

Who Could That Be at This Hour?

By Lemony Snicket. Illus. by Seth. Little, Brown, 2012. 272p. Ages 8-12

Snicket, author of the popular Series of Unfortunate Events stories, presents the first book of the projected four-volume All the Wrong Questions series, providing "autobiographical" accounts of his unconventional childhood. As the book opens, twelve-year-old Lemony Snicket takes his first case as apprentice to chaperone S. Theodora Markson. They have been hired to retrieve a vastly valuable statue of the local legend, the Bombinating Beast. This fast-paced whodunit, filled with droll humor, wordplay, literary allusions, and quirky characters, will thrill readers of the Series of Unfortunate Events series and attract new fans.

Winnie Years: Ten
(Winnie Years series)

By Lauren Myracle. Dutton, 2011. 272p. Ages 10-12

This prequel to the other books in the Winnie Years series adds backstory to Winnie's tweenhood; *Eleven* (2004), *Twelve* (2007), and *Thirteen* (2008) fill in the Winnie Years between ages ten and fourteen. At ten, Winnie celebrates with a haunted house–themed birthday party; the ensuing year is filled with everytween episodes (each chapter represents one month in the year after she turns ten) such as making mistakes, coping with bullies, getting support from friends, and more.

Winnie Years: Thirteen plus One
(Winnie Years series)

By Lauren Myracle. Dutton, 2010. 304p. Ages 10-12

Winnie turns fourteen and is stressed out: her big sister is leaving for college, her boyfriend does not seem to "get her," and soon, she will be a confused freshman in high school. Spending her summer at a wildlife preservation camp, Winnie learns that to avoid being disappointed, she needs to clearly express what she really wants. Breezy, hilarious, and warm, with some solid pieces of life wisdom dotting the way, Winnie's tale is a surefire winner for tween girls.

Wonder

By R. J. Palacio. Knopf, 2012. 320p. (DC) Ages 9-13

Ten-year-old Auggie Pullman was born with severe facial deformities, and even after twenty-seven surgeries to correct what doctors refer to as "anomalies," he's learned to steel himself against the horrified reactions he receives from people. After years of homeschooling, Auggie is about to start fifth grade. The story of his first year at school unfolds from the first-person perspectives of family members, classmates, and Auggie himself, expressing the impact of this experience on him and everyone in his community. Readers will be moved and inspired by Auggie's humor, intelligence, courage, and kindness.

The Wonder of Charlie Anne

By Kimberly Newton Fusco. Knopf, 2010. 256p. (DC) Ages 10-13

Dramatic first-person narration presents Charlie Anne's small-town Massachusetts life during the Great Depression: she misses her lyrical mama who recently died during childbirth, she locks horns with cousin Mirabel who moved in to help, she misses papa and brother Thomas when they take road-building jobs to save their farm, she does endless chores to put food on the table, and she cannot read. Her neighbor's new wife moves in with an adopted "colored" daughter Phoebe who is the perfect friend for Charlie Anne once they bridge a racial divide. Charlie Anne helps others overcome racial misconceptions and also learns to read.

Wonderstruck

By Brian Selznick. Scholastic, 2011. 640p. Ages 9-13

Two parallel stories set fifty years apart intertwine in this fast-paced illustrated novel. The first story, set in 1977 in Gunflint Lake, Minnesota, is told in prose and follows Ben, who never knew his father and is grieving the recent loss of his mother. The second, told through illustrations, is set in 1927 in Hoboken, New Jersey, and follows Rose, who runs away to New York in search of her silent film–star mother. Eventually, the two stories converge at the American Museum of Natural History. Although hefty, at more than six hundred pages, this mesmerizes; once they begin, readers will find it difficult to put down.

Wonkenstein

By Obert Skye. Holt/Christy Ottaviano, 2011. 240p. Ages 9-12

Rob's closet is an incubator for disaster—literally. A former makeshift lab, it is packed with unwanted stuff, including the books his mother is constantly giving him to read. The closet has an unusually heavy door and a creepy doorknob with an engraving of a smiling bearded man who always seems to be watching Rob. When Wonk—a creature that's part Willy Wonka, part Frankenstein's monster—emerges from his closet, Rob undertakes outrageous schemes and madcap chases to get Wonk back home. Playful illustrations complement the fast-paced narrative.

Zora and Me

By Victoria Bond and T. R. Simon. Candlewick, 2010. 192p. (DC) Ages 10-13

Meet young Zora Neale Hurston and her best friends Carrie and Teddy, growing up in Eatonville, Florida, during the early 1900s. Zora's future as a writer is presaged by her childhood talent: she is a collector of stories and is always in search of new ones, even when they land her in trouble. Mysteries abound in Eatonville, from the sinister "Gator Man" to an unsolved murder, in this fictionalized biography. CORETTA SCOTT KING AUTHOR HONOR BOOK

Informational Books

Recommendations for cultivating a diverse collection are indicated by "(DC)."

100 Things You Should Know about Elephants

By Camilla de la Bédoyère. Mason Crest, 2011. 48p. Ages 6-12

One hundred facts about elephants are presented in twenty-one chapters on double-page spreads. Beautiful paintings and photographs with simple, fluid text cover the elephant's gentle disposition, ancestry, natural habitats, intelligence, physical and social characteristics and grim future due to poaching. Readers are encouraged to study elephants through research, reading, and tourism. A table of contents and index provide access points and brief quizzes and boxes of additional facts are included in this book for students in grades three through six reading for research or recreation, and curious prereaders.

Abraham Lincoln & Frederick Douglass: The Story behind an American Friendship

By Russell Freedman. Clarion, 2012. 128p. (DC) Ages 10-14

One man fought to free slaves; the other escaped from slavery to free himself. These two towering figures in American history met only three times, but their lives were forever entwined by the times in which they lived. And while much is known of Lincoln, less is known of Douglass, and this side-by-side look at their lives places both men within the context of the familiar and known and fosters a more complete understanding of the times. Carefully chosen period illustrations and excellent back matter complete this fine example of informational writing.

Actual Times: America Is Under Attack: The Day the Towers Fell
(Actual Times series)

By Don Brown. Illus. by the author. Roaring Brook/Flash Point, 2011. 32p. Ages 6–10

The fourth installment in the Actual Times series presents a chronological account of the September 11, 2001, terrorist attacks on the World Trade Center in New York City and the Pentagon in Washington, DC, and the hijacking of a plane that crashed in Shanksville, Pennsylvania. The elegantly written text describes the heroic deeds of the victims and survivors. Color illustrations are somber, realistic, and appropriate. Back matter includes an author's note, a bibliography, and source notes.

Amelia Lost: The Life and Disappearance of Amelia Earhart

By Candace Fleming. Random/Schwartz & Wade, 2011. 128p. Ages 10–14

Parallel narratives, one a biography of the aviator and the other a gripping account of her final flight and the ensuing search, alternate to weave together a compelling portrait. Maps, archival documents and photos, and frequent sidebars keep things lively and make this appropriate for browsers as well as researchers, or just interested readers.

Annie and Helen

By Deborah Hopkinson. Illus. by Raul Colón. Random/Schwartz & Wade, 2012. 48p. (DC) Ages 7–10

This compelling account with a deceptively simple title opens with the introduction of seven-year-old Helen Keller to her new teacher, then twenty-one-year-old Annie Sullivan, a relationship that lasted nearly fifty years. The scope here is appropriately limited, though; the action closes once Helen is able to write her mother a letter, a major achievement. The spare, clear text is enhanced by soft watercolor illustrations suitable to the period and that humanize the challenges and euphoria inherent in successfully teaching someone who cannot hear, speak, or see to communicate effectively. End-papers feature photos of the two women, and back matter includes a raised braille alphabet and a bibliography.

The Beetle Book
By Steve Jenkins. Illus. by the author. Houghton Mifflin Harcourt, 2012. 32p. Ages 8-12

Did you know that if you line up every kind of plant and animal on earth, one out of every four will be a beetle? Beetles in all sizes, shapes, and colors are featured in this informative introduction that covers what they are, what makes them unique, their physical features and development, and how they communicate, fight, and disguise themselves. Engaging, colorful collages illustrate the creatures in larger-than-life detail on a clean white background. Concluding information includes Latin names, the part of the world where they are found, and the size and length for each beetle listed.

Big Wig: A Little History of Hair
By Kathleen Krull. Illus. by Peter Malone. Scholastic/Arthur A. Levine, 2011. 48p. (DC) Ages 7-11

The history of human hair styles is presented with snippets of information adorned with amusing and distinguished oil paintings. Modern and ancient connections link present-day cornrows with life in Nigeria five thousand years ago, the Supremes' and Marge Simpson's hair with Marie Antoinette's hair sculptures built around a wire frame, today's punk look with do's worn by Scottish warriors three thousand years ago, and much more. Anyone fascinated with hair will appreciate these well-researched facts accompanied by notes and a bibliography.

Bomb: The Race to Build—and Steal—the World's Most Dangerous Weapon
By Steve Sheinkin. Roaring Brook/Flash Point, 2012. 272p. Ages 10-14

This gripping account of the international race to create the first atomic weapon opens with Soviet spy Harry Gold as he is about to be apprehended by the FBI on charges of espionage. This scene becomes the backstory for the rest of the narrative as it unfolds, revealing the Soviet infiltration of the laboratories at Los Alamos, where the scientists of the Manhattan project, led by Robert Oppenheimer, worked to develop the most lethal weapon in history. Also highlighted is the heroism of Knut Haukelid, who parachuted into Norway to destroy Germany's heavy-water plant, preventing the Germans from attaining the bomb toward the end of World War II. Written with journalistic immediacy, this reads like a thriller but maintains historical accuracy. The narrative reminds young historians of the long-term impact of the atomic bomb on subsequent generations and of continuing concerns about the use of nuclear energy. Includes archival photographs, primary source documents, comprehensive source notes, an annotated bibliography, photo credits, and an index. NEWBERY HONOR BOOK, SIBERT MEDAL

Bones: Skeletons and How They Work

By Steve Jenkins. Illus. by the author. Scholastic, 2010. 48p. Ages 7-10

No bones about it, this book will engage readers! Kids are fascinated by bones. They encounter bones in the food they eat, Halloween skeletons, broken bones, and more. Beginning with one bone (one of twenty-six bones in a human hand), the exploration continues to the human arm, then a comparison with other animals, explaining the similarities and differences of bone structure and function. Cut-paper collage illustrations are striking against solid-color backgrounds and most are actual size. Gatefolds (animal skulls, human, python) display the skeletons of these creatures. Fascinating back matter includes bone facts, stories, and the history and science of bones.

Bootleg: Murder, Moonshine, and the Lawless Years of Prohibition

By Karen Blumenthal. Roaring Brook/Flash Point, 2011. 160p. Ages 13-14

Here is the comprehensive story of the Eighteenth Amendment, which banned the manufacture, transport, sale, and consumption of alcohol. Blumenthal sets the context for her examination of the Prohibition era by exploring America's historic relationship with alcohol from colonial times to the present day, including the origins and development of the temperance movement. An engaging fast-paced narrative, period art and photographs, reproductions of propaganda material, anecdotes, and portraits of unique characters of the time, such as Al Capone, bring the era to life. This relevant, timely title includes a glossary, an extensive bibliography, source notes, and an index.

Bring on the Birds

By Susan Stockdale. Illus. by the author. Peachtree, 2011. 32p. Ages 3-7

Budding ornithologists will appreciate this colorful, bountiful array of all kinds of birds, including ones that don't fly, ones that swim, and more. Exotic species such as peacocks, ostriches, and penguins are covered, as is the everyday pigeon. Bright, clear acrylic paintings bring the animals to life in one double-page spread per bird; back matter provides further details about each one as well as a bibliography for further reading.

A Butterfly Is Patient

By Dianna Hutts Aston. Illus. by Sylvia Long. Chronicle, 2011. 40p. Ages 7-9

Do you *really* understand the steps a caterpillar takes to become a butterfly? Following the format of *An Egg is Quiet* (2006) and *A Seed is Sleepy* (2007), here is a beautiful portrayal of the caterpillar-to-butterfly transformation. The text focuses on the development, habits, sizes, features, defense mechanisms, and migration of butterflies; soft, detailed, and warm beautiful watercolor illustrations bring this fascinating process to life.

Can We Save the Tiger?

By Martin Jenkins. Illus. by Vicky White. Candlewick, 2011. 56p. Ages 5-9

Frank prose and compelling sketchbook-style illustrations explain wildlife conservation and animal extinction. Design elements such as varying font sizes, contrasting image sizes and styles, and distinctive page layouts help to make complex issues accessible. The clear text and honest observations help children understand why what makes tigers special also makes them endangered. Less beautiful animals, like snails and vultures, are included as well as examples of efforts that are making a difference.

Chuck Close: Face Book

By Chuck Close. Abrams, 2012. 64p. Ages 8-12

Creative design elements, a compelling personal history, and immediacy granted by conveying information in the form of interviews with fifth-grade kids characterize this fascinating biography of artist Close. Close overcame a number of challenges, including dyslexia in childhood and a stroke as an adult, to pursue his calling, and young readers and artists may be called to try their hand at "face books" themselves.

Disasters: Natural and Man-Made Catastrophes through the Centuries

By Brenda Z. Guiberson. Illus. by the author. Holt/Christy Ottaviano, 2010. 240p. Ages 10-13

This intriguing collection takes readers around the world and back in time to revisit some of the most tragic events in written history. Epidemics, hurricanes, icebergs, and more are examined with care, and readers are left knowing how human nature affects such events for better or worse. Familiar events, such as the *Titanic* sinking, are reported with fresh insights, and excellent back matter completes this fine example of informational writing.

Drawing from Memory

By Allen Say. Illus. by the author. Scholastic, 2011. 64p. (DC) Ages 10-12

While growing up in Japan, Say was discouraged by his father from drawing and aspiring to become a cartoon artist. At twelve, Say had his own apartment and studied with master cartoonist sensei Noro Shinpei during World War II. This memoir portrays a determined young man who stuck to his dreams and honors his mentor to this day. Photographs and comics are interwoven throughout the text, making this account especially memorable. SIBERT HONOR BOOK

The Good, the Bad, and the Barbie: A Doll's History and Her Impact on Us

By Tanya Lee Stone. Viking, 2010. 136p. Ages 10-14

The perennially popular Barbie Doll has enjoyed praises and endured resentment for many decades. Backed by solid research, here is a mostly positive look at the history of Barbie, its creator and producers, and the doll's societal impact. This thoroughly fun and engrossing informational read features an attention-grabbing cover, many passionate first-person anecdotes, and colorful photographs with enlightening captions.

Hand in Hand: Ten Black Men Who Changed America

By Andrea Davis Pinkney. Illus. by Brian Pinkney. Disney/Jump at the Sun, 2012. 243p. (DC) Ages 9-13

This celebration of black male achievement presents ten accounts of the lives and contributions of influential African American men from varied eras and walks of life who made significant impacts on American history.

Chronologically organized, the men profiled include Benjamin Banneker, Frederick Douglass, Booker T. Washington, W. E. B. DuBois, A. Philip Randolph, Thurgood Marshall, Jackie Robinson, Malcolm X, Martin Luther King Jr., and Barack Obama. Dramatic watercolor portraits illuminate the achievements of these larger-than-life figures.

Heart and Soul: The Story of America and African Americans

By Kadir Nelson. Illus. by the author. HarperCollins/Balzer + Bray, 2011. 108p. (DC) Ages 9-12

Beginning with slavery and ending with the present, the first-person narration from the point of view of an elderly African American woman tells an engaging and informative story integrating African Americans into America's history. The story covers major events such as World Wars I and II, Reconstruction, the Great Migration, the civil rights era, and many others. Stunning oil paintings convey both the dignity of the people and the horror of how they were treated. CORETTA SCOTT KING AUTHOR AWARD AND ILLUSTRATOR HONOR BOOK

How They Croaked: The Awful Ends of the Awfully Famous

By Georgia Bragg. Illus. by Kevin O'Malley. Walker, 2011. 192p. Ages 10-13

History books usually tell about a person's life but not always their death, especially if it was gross, gory, or just plain weird. *How They Croaked* changes all that. Readers learn a little about the lives of nineteen famous dead people and everything about their deaths: what happened, who caused it, and every squeamish detail. Learn how a sore throat killed one of the greatest composers ever or how one bad tooth took the life of our first president. Irreverent illustrations just add to this fun, factual, and deadly serious book.

I Have a Dream: Dr. Martin Luther King, Jr.

By Martin Luther King Jr. Illus. by Kadir Nelson. Random/Schwartz & Wade, 2012. 40p. (DC) Ages 5-8

This is a fiftieth anniversary tribute to the civil rights leader and the inspirational speech he delivered on August 28, 1963, at the Lincoln Memorial during the March on Washington. Luminous oil paintings illuminate King's ideals and include portraits of King and scenes from the event, accompanying actual text from one of the most powerful and memorable speeches in US history. The complete text of the speech is appended. Also included is a CD of King's address. CORETTA SCOTT KING ILLUSTRATOR HONOR BOOK

The Impossible Rescue: The True Story of an Amazing Arctic Adventure

By Martin W. Sandler. Candlewick, 2012. 176p. Ages 10-14

In this gripping, true story, we meet men and women who braved—and even thrived in—the Arctic. When the seas froze early in 1897, eight whaling ships became trapped, leaving the crews in grave danger. A single ship escaped and delivered news of the crisis, and the American government planned a daring rescue. Without the modern conveniences of fleece, or snowmobiles, a team of men began a perilous 1,500-mile journey to bring food and supplies to the trapped ships. Along the way, Alaskan Natives and traders shared invaluable knowledge and resources to make this "impossible rescue" possible.

Island: A Story of the Galápagos

By Jason Chin. Illus. by the author. Roaring Brook/Neal Porter, 2012. 40p. Ages 5-9

The fascinating biology, geology, and history of these islands, famous as the place that harbored the right variety of species to demonstrate the theory of evolution, is portrayed here in sumptuously detailed illustrations and a perhaps too-brief text. This will undoubtedly whet the appetite of young naturalists, however; and more information is noted in the back matter, divided into three sections: about Darwin, about the islands themselves, and about the species that live there.

Mammoths and Mastodons: Titans of the Ice Age

By Cheryl Bardoe. Abrams, 2010. 48p. Ages 9-12

When two kids in Siberia found a frozen skeleton of a baby woolly mammoth in 2007, it provided new clues for scientists piecing together the fascinating world of these extinct elephant relatives. Clear explanations of scientific methods and quotations from modern experts in the field are supported by diagrams, photographs, and paintings, showing how today's scientists use everything from "tusk rings" to "droppings" to develop new theories about the ways that mammoths and mastodons lived more than ten thousand years ago.

Moonbird: A Year on the Wind with the Great Survivor B95

By Phillip Hoose. Farrar, 2012. 160p. Ages 10-14

This documents the survival tale of a shorebird that in its twenty-year lifetime has made an 18,000 mile annual migratory circuit between Argentina and the Canadian Arctic. Scientists call him Moonbird because over the course of this lifetime, he has flown more than 325,000 miles, the distance from the earth to the moon and nearly halfway back. The bird's physiology, migratory paths, flight patterns, feeding habits, and habitats are covered, and budding ornithologists are introduced to a worldwide team of scientists and conservationists that are trying to save this endangered species. Includes photographs, maps, diagrams, numerous informative sidebars, comprehensive source notes, an extensive bibliography, and an index.

Nic Bishop Snakes

By Nic Bishop. Illus. by the author. Scholastic Nonfiction, 2012. 48p. Ages 5-9

As in previous titles such as *Nic Bishop Lizards* (2010), here, the close-up, full-color photographs take center stage. General information about snakes includes how many species there are (3,000), where they live (every continent except Antarctica), and more; numerous individual species are introduced in much greater, fascinating detail. Back matter includes an index, a bibliography, and an author's note about the challenges of herpetological photography.

The Notorious Benedict Arnold: A True Story of Adventure, Heroism, & Treachery

By Steve Sheinkin. Roaring Brook/Flash Point, 2010. 352p. Ages 10-14

Most people think they know the story of Benedict Arnold—a cowardly man who betrayed his country and was the worst kind of traitor. Here, readers learn that Arnold was one of America's first war heroes and a personal friend of George Washington. Gripping writing, suspense, and eye-opening first-person accounts take readers through the career of General Arnold, first as a man the Rebels could not do without, and then as one they wanted nothing to do with. This stunning account of his life and fall guarantees that young historians will never view Benedict Arnold the same way again.

Ocean Sunlight: How Tiny Plants Feed the Seas

By Molly Bang and Penny Chisholm. Illus. by Molly Bang. Scholastic/Blue Sky, 2012. 48p.
Ages 6-8

The sun narrates this account itself, explaining how the "tiny plants," or phytoplankton, make up a key part of the food chain and also provide half the oxygen on earth. Intricately detailed paintings show the interconnectedness of all creatures, from the smallest to the largest in the sea. The science here is sophisticated and may need some additional explanation, but it's fascinating.

Older than the Stars

By Karen C. Fox. Illus. by Nancy Davis. Charlesbridge, 2010. 32p. Ages 7-10

This cumulative story tells of how the earth was formed billions of years ago by cosmic dust, volatile gases, and an explosive BANG. Vibrant colors and shifting shapes build excitement while depicting the powerful forces that created our planet. We are also reminded that the same elements that shaped our world all those eons ago are still active within us even today.

Orangutans Are Ticklish: Fun Facts from an Animal Photographer

By Steve Grubman and Jill Davis. Illus. by Steve Grubman. Random/Schwartz & Wade, 2010. 40p. Ages 6-9

Did you know that a hippo's yawn doesn't mean she's tired? It means she wants to fight! Vibrant close-up photographs, fascinating facts about the animal kingdom, and behind-the-scenes stories about how animal photographs are taken characterize this introduction to animals such as the hippopotamus, aardvark, western gray kangaroo, grizzly bear, chimpanzee, lion, tiger, alligator, orangutan, elephant, giraffe, coatimundi, and zebra. This will intrigue animal lovers, young scientists, and budding photographers.

Saga of the Sioux: An Adaptation of Dee Brown's *Bury My Heart at Wounded Knee* *Bury My Heart at Wounded Knee*

By Dwight Jon Zimmerman. Holt, 2011. 240p. (DC) Ages 10-14

This adaptation of the groundbreaking *Bury My Heart at Wounded Knee* makes one of the most tragic periods in American history accessible for younger readers. The original 1970 publication was one of the first to address the removal of the Native Americans from their lands from the Native perspective and was all the more powerful for its use of primary source materials. Here, the focus is narrowed to the plight of the Sioux, featuring Sioux perspective and terminology.

Saving Audie: A Pit Bull Puppy Gets a Second Chance

By Dorothy Hinshaw Patent. Illus. by William Muñoz. Walker, 2011. 40p. Ages 7-9

Audie was one of dozens of pit bulls rescued from the infamous dog-fighting ring owned by football player Michael Vick. After placement in a new home, Audie's background required attending canine classes and learning how to trust, play, and get along with other dogs and humans. Color photos depict Audie's journey to redemption owing to patience and love by the humans who rescue him. Animal-loving children will be empathetic to Audie's plight and will cheer his progress. Back matter includes information about the breed, rescue groups, a timeline about the Vick case, and further resources.

Sit-In: How Four Friends Stood Up by Sitting Down

By Andrea Davis Pinkney. Illus. by Brian Pinkney. Little, Brown, 2010. 40p. (DC) Ages 6-10

The sit-ins of the civil rights era may seem like ancient history to contemporary kids; this package of easy-to-read poetic text and loose, colorful artwork portrays one specific event and also puts it into context among other happenings nationwide. Here, four African American college students sit in at a Woolworth's lunch counter, expecting only to be treated fairly and served lunch as the white customers are. Exemplifying the movement's emphasis on nonviolence, they still had to be ready for anything; their courage inspires today. A timeline and a bibliography offer additional information.

A Strange Place to Call Home: The World's Most Dangerous Habitats and the Animals That Call Them Home

By Marilyn Singer. Illus. by Ed Young. Chronicle, 2012. 44p. Ages 6-8

Poetry and natural history combine here to cover a fascinating topic: habitats that would seem at first to be actually dangerous to the animals that live in them. Fourteen animals are discussed, including blind cave fish, snow monkeys, mountain goats, and more; the variety of poetic forms and textured paper collage illustrations keep things interesting.

Suryia and Roscoe: The True Story of an Unlikely Friendship

By Bhagavan Antle and Thea Feldman. Holt, 2011. 32p. Ages 4-8

Suryia is an orangutan. Roscoe is a stray dog. And from the day they meet, they become unlikely best friends. Text and color photographs depict the blooming of their friendship at a South Carolina wildlife preserve and some of their favorite activities together. Even as children find the real-life friendship incredible, they are immediately drawn to the charming photos of Suryia and Roscoe hugging, romping, swimming, and even mugging for the camera. Consider themes of friendship, conservation, or endangered animals when sharing this title with older preschoolers and elementary students.

Titanic: Voices from the Disaster

By Deborah Hopkinson. Scholastic, 2012. 304p. Ages 9-13

A nine-year-old boy, a millionaire, and a heroic wireless operator are among the many people whose words and experiences come to life in this riveting account of the Titanic disaster. Using first-hand accounts, photos from the period, and a fascinating collection of facts and statistics, the author brings the reader right into the historical drama of the historical events. Along with the suspense and action, the multiple points of view lead to questions about class relations, the nature of courage, and other thought-provoking issues.

Treasury of Greek Mythology: Classic Stories of Gods, Goddesses, Heroes & Monsters

By Donna Jo Napoli. Illus. by Christina Balit. National Geographic, 2011. 192p. Ages 10-14

Twenty-five major figures in Greek mythology are introduced in a lively, vivid style, and a dramatically illustrated Olympus family tree opens the collection. Each figure's origins and legendary story are featured and illuminated with striking artwork. Informative sidebars appear throughout the text, providing historical, cultural, and scientific information. Helpful back matter includes thumbnail portraits for the "cast of characters," a map of Greece, a timeline, a bibliographic note, an index, and lists of recommended books and websites.

What's New, Cupcake? Ingeniously Simple Designs for Every Occasion

By Karen Tack and Alan Richardson. Houghton Mifflin Harcourt, 2010. 240p. Ages 10-14

Detailed instructions and colorful photographs illustrate each tasty and creative cupcake recipe, making it easy to design the different works of "edible art." While many of the projects are complex, the "EZ Cupcakes" feature showcases projects that are significantly simpler, and several are included in each chapter. Designs include picnic ants, sub sandwiches, rubber ducks, and turkey drumsticks. Put this in a young chef's hands and see what masterpieces he or she creates!

Who Was Rosa Parks?
(Who Was . . . ? series)

By Yona Zeldis McDonough. Illus. by Steven Marchesi. Grosset & Dunlap, 2010. 112p. (DC)
Ages 8-12

Short chapters and drawings describe Rosa McCauley's childhood experiences with segregation, Klu Klux Klan violence, and her determination to complete high school and become a registered voter. Volunteer work with the National Association for the Advancement of Colored People (NAACP) combined with family support gave her the courage to be arrested for remaining seated in the colored section of a Montgomery bus and to go to court to have the law overturned. Parks became a spokesperson for civil rights and social justice and continued to dedicate her life to these efforts. Related historical summaries, a timeline, and a bibliography are in this entry to the compelling, fact-packed Who Was . . . ? series.

The Wimpy Kid Movie Diary: How Greg Heffley Went Hollywood

By Jeff Kinney. Illus. by the author. Abrams/Amulet, 2010. 208p. Ages 10-13

Kids love *Diary of a Wimpy Kid*, first as the popular book series and now movies. Wimpy Kid author Jeff Kinney shares his experiences on the set of the first movie, explaining the ins and outs of film production, from concept to casting to special effects. (Devoted fans go straight to how they made the cheese for the dreaded cheese touch.) The familiar format of notebook pages and sketches is enhanced by numerous color photos from the set, providing an intimate view guaranteed to fascinate Wimpy fans and budding auteurs alike.

Graphic Novels

Recommendations for cultivating a diverse collection are indicated by "(DC)."

Amelia Rules! Her Permanent Record
(Amelia Rules! series)

By Jimmy Gownley. Illus. by the author. Simon & Schuster/Atheneum, 2012. 160p.
Ages 9-12

This is the final series entry, and fans won't be disappointed. This time, Amelia and her friends set out to find out what has happened to Amelia's Aunt Tanner, who had been on a book tour with her boyfriend when Amelia abruptly disappeared.

Amelia Rules! Superheroes
(Amelia Rules! series)

By Jimmy Gownley. Illus. by the author. Simon & Schuster/Atheneum, 2011. 176p. Ages 9-12

School may be out, but the tween drama continues: Truth or Dare?, a friend's secret, and the possibility of her family's moving have Amelia in a tizzy. Realistic situations and dialogue conveyed in a kid-friendly, graphic format make this series of stories especially accessible.

Amelia Rules! The Meaning of Life . . . and Other Stuff
(Amelia Rules! series)

By Jimmy Gownley. Illus. by the author. Simon & Schuster/Atheneum, 2011. 160p. Ages 9-12

Amelia and her friends are growing up and are about to start middle school. Middle school is a challenging time for many kids, and Amelia's no exception; it's hard to cope with cheerleading, crushes, impending puberty, and more. The situations will ring true for Amelia's legion of fans.

Amelia Rules! The Tweenage Guide to Not Being Unpopular
(Amelia Rules! series)

By Jimmy Gownley. Illus. by the author. Simon & Schuster/Atheneum, 2010. 192p. Ages 9-12

Amelia is having a hard time navigating the increasingly roiling waters of elementary school friendship. In their quest to figure out how to be cool, Amelia and her crew try out different hairstyles and even new friends. But things backfire, and Amelia ends up realizing that popularity may not be so important after all. This deft combination of humor and realism creates a thought-provoking story that rings true, alongside colorfully comic illustrations.

Amelia Rules! The Whole World's Crazy
(Amelia Rules! series)

By Jimmy Gownley. Illus. by the author. Simon & Schuster/Atheneum, 2011. 176p. Ages 9-12

This is the first installment of the Amelia Rules! series, although it wasn't the first one to be reissued commercially after the books' original self-publication. When Amelia's parents divorce, she must adjust to life outside Manhattan in a generic small town. Fortunately, it is here that she meets her now familiar posse of friends: Reggie, Rhonda, and Pajamaman.

Amelia Rules! True Things (Adults Don't Want Kids to Know)
(Amelia Rules! series)

By Jimmy Gownley. Illus. by the author. Simon & Schuster/Atheneum, 2010. 176p. Ages 9-12

Amelia's got to cope with some adult-sized issues now that she's turning eleven, when her Aunt Tanner starts dating Amelia's teacher, and Tanner and Amelia's mom start to argue. Her friends are arguing too, and an intense crush doesn't make things easier. Perennial tween issues are dealt with here with honesty and humor.

Amelia Rules! What Makes You Happy
(Amelia Rules! series)

By Jimmy Gownley. Illus. by the author. Simon & Schuster/Atheneum, 2011. 176p. Ages 9-12

Amelia's adjusting to being the new kid in school, and she and her friends are learning more about her mysterious Aunt Tanner, who might be a rock star. Everytween experiences are treated honestly and with humor here, as in other series entries.

Amelia Rules! When the Past Is a Present
(Amelia Rules! series)

By Jimmy Gownley. Illus. by the author. Simon & Schuster/Atheneum, 2011. 176p. Ages 9-12

The "present" here is a box of old photos that Amelia discovers; the "past" is what she learns about family. Amelia's now ten years old and is encountering some increasingly weighty issues: a friend's military father is being shipped out, and Amelia has her first crush.

Amulet: Prince of the Elves
(Amulet series)

By Kazu Kibuishi. Illus. by the author. Scholastic/Graphix, 2010. 208p. Ages 11-14

Character driven as well as plot (adventure) driven, this engrossing entry in the Amulet series is set as war approaches between humans and elves. Following on the story arc first introduced in *The Stonekeeper* (2007), this fleshes out the backstory of Emily and Nevin.

Amulet: The Cloud Searchers
(Amulet series)

By Kazu Kibuishi. Illus. by the author. Scholastic/Graphix, 2010. 208p. Ages 11-14

In the third volume of the Amulet series, Emily and her allies go in search of the lost city of Cielis, the last known location of the Guardian Council. Along the way, they enlist the aid of Trellis and Luger, who have their own reasons for wanting to see the Elf King fall. Kibuishi's artwork is beautiful, particularly the full-page watercolor spreads, which may lull people into thinking this story is for younger children. But this story is a fully realized hero's quest, complete with action, violence, and introspection and will thoroughly satisfy high fantasy lovers; the saga continues in *The Last Council* (2011) and *Prince of the Elves* (2012).

Amulet: The Last Council
(Amulet series)

By Kazu Kibuishi. Illus. by the author. Scholastic/Graphix, 2011. 224p. Ages 9-11

Blending a strong plotline, a clear text, and luscious illustrations, the fourth installment of the Amulet series brings Emily and her cohorts to Cielis, the home of the Guardian Council of Stonekeepers. Believing they could find help in this legendary city to defeat the Elf King, they instead discover a deserted city infested with terrible secrets. When Emily is forced into a competition among young Stonekeepers to secure a seat on the Guardian Council, she learns that not only her own life but the safety of the whole world is at stake.

Anya's Ghost

By Vera Brogsol. Illus. by the author. First Second, 2011. 224p. Ages 12-14

Growing up with her single mother and younger brother, Anya tries to fit in, and she distances herself from geeky, "fresh off the boat" Dima, another Russian immigrant at her school. After accidentally falling down an abandoned well, Anya meets a ghost named Emily, who claims to be a murder victim that has been dead and trapped inside for the past ninety years. Anya and Emily become "friends" until Anya learns that her ghostly companion has a darker agenda. The mix of mystery, horror, and everyday high school concerns in this debut graphic novel produce a very engaging story, with particular appeal for reluctant readers.

Around the World

By Matt Phelan. Illus. by the author. Candlewick, 2011. 240p. Ages 11-14

Thomas Stevens, first to ride a bicycle around the world; Nellie Bly, first to race around the world and beat the record set in Jules Verne's *Around the World in Eighty Days*; and Joshua Slocum, first to sail around the world by himself have gone down in history as three of America's most intrepid adventurers. In three consecutive stories, armchair globetrotters imagine the motivations, both private and public, that led each to accomplish his or her feat. The pen-and-pencil line drawings are remarkably expressive, and the watercolor washes give a romantic air to these more-true-than-not stories.

Bad Island

By Doug TenNapel. Illus. by the author. Scholastic/Graphix, 2011. 224p. Ages 11-14

No one but dad is particularly interested in going on the planned family vacation, especially teenage Reese, who is desperate to stay home alone. When their boat gets caught in a freak storm and shipwrecks on an island inhabited by strange creatures, Reese has to step up and help protect his parents, his snake-obsessed little sister, and the strange artifact the bad guys are after. This hefty story told with vibrant, somewhat chaotic artwork gives readers complex ideas to think about regarding family and father-son relationships.

Bake Sale

By Sara Varon. Illus. by the author. First Second, 2011. 160p. Ages 8-10

Bakery owner Cupcake is in a rut. He's tired of making the same recipes and new ones just aren't working for him. Offered a chance to travel to Turkey to meet a famous pastry chef, Cupcake sacrifices all his spare time to earn enough money to take the trip. But when his best friend falls on hard times, Cupcake has to decide what's most important to him, meeting his hero or helping his friend. Charming, deceptively simple artwork makes this slow-paced, gently profound story accessible to younger readers while satisfying older ones. Recipes are also included.

The Big Adventures of Majoko (Vol. 3)
(Big Adventures of Majoko series)

By Tomomi Mizuna. Illus. by the author. Udon, 2010. 200p. Ages 11-14

Manga meets vampires and princesses in this volume of the Big Adventures of Majoko. Majoko herself tangles with a vampire, and her human friend Nana becomes a real-life princess.

The Big Adventures of Majoko (Vol. 4)
(Big Adventures of Majoko series)

By Tomomi Mizuna. Illus. by the author. Udon, 2010. 200p. Ages 11-14

Majoko and Nana are back, and while this volume of the Big Adventures of Majoko isn't completely Christmas themed, they do meet Santa. Young readers with fond memories of Candyland and their youthful train fascinations will be excited by the girls' trip to the land of sweets and their ride on a magical train.

The Big Adventures of Majoko (Vol. 5)
(Big Adventures of Majoko series)

By Tomomi Mizuna. Illus. by the author. Udon, 2011. 200p. Ages 11–14

When Majoko, a young witch from the Land of Magic, comes looking for a human playmate, a world of adventure opens up for her new friend Nana. Together the two explore the different areas that make up the Land of Magic while getting in and out of trouble. Each chapter is a stand-alone story, but characters reappear and jokes build, rewarding faithful readers of the series. The artwork is basic big-eyed-girl-style manga, staying clear and making the story easy to follow for readers new to reading from right to left.

Bigfoot Boy: Into the Woods
(Bigfoot Boy series)

By J. Torres. Illus. by Faith Erin Hicks. Kids Can, 2012. 100p. Ages 8–12

Rufus thinks a weekend spent with his grandmother is going to be super boring, but when he finds a strange amulet in the woods and recites the incantation carved into it, things take a turn toward the adventuresome: he turns into a Sasquatch. Rufus thinks it's pretty cool being big, hairy, and able to talk to animals, but some of the animals aren't thrilled about the shift in the balance of power and plot to get the amulet back. While not full of surprises, the plot is simple enough for younger readers to follow and exciting enough to keep older readers on board for the next volume in the new Bigfoot Boy series.

Broxo

By Zack Giallongo. Illus. by the author. First Second, 2012. 240p. Ages 10–14

When young Princess Zora goes in search of a lost tribe of barbarians, she finds only Broxo, the last of his kind, who lives alone with his huge white beast, Migo. They join forces to find out what happened to Broxo's tribe, while fighting off the undead "creepers" that emerge from the nearby swamp. The provocative artwork depicts graphic consequences of violence in this epic fantasy full of swords, sorcery, witches, and battles.

Cardboard

By Doug TenNapel. Illus. by the author. Scholastic/Graphix, 2012. 288p. Ages 9–13

A 75-cent cardboard box seems like the worst birthday present ever until Cam discovers that he can use it to bring a cardboard man to life in this imaginative graphic novel. Cam's fun times with his newly created friend end when a jealous neighbor kid steals the magical cardboard, makes his own "creature factory," and unleashes an army of uncontrollable monsters. Paneled artwork depicts dramatic scenes of action and emotion as Cam and his friends try to stop the cardboard creatures from taking over their town.

Chi's Sweet Home (Vol. 1)
(Chi's Sweet Home series)
By Konami Kanata. Illus. by the author. Vertical, 2010. 144p. Ages 8-12

When Chi, a kitten who gets separated from her mother while visiting a local park, is adopted by the Yamada family, both she and the Yamadas must learn to get along while sharing an apartment that doesn't allow pets. Any pet owner will recognize the true-to-life catness of Chi—her single-mindedness, her ability to sleep anywhere, and her love of boxes and paper bags—and want to read more. This ongoing series is in full color and has been "flipped" to read left-to-right, making it a great choice for beginning manga readers. The series continues through volume 9 (2012) and likely beyond.

Chi's Sweet Home (Vol. 2)
(Chi's Sweet Home series)
By Konami Kanata. Illus. by the author. Vertical, 2010. 144p. Ages 8-12

Kitten Chi and toddler Yohei are still getting to know one another in the second volume of Chi's Sweet Home. This time, Chi learns about human bath time, various human foods, and how to share bed space, toys, and more with her human "sibling." A particularly touching scene shows Chi wondering what sleeping cuddled next to Yohei reminds her of; once she falls asleep, a bubble revealing her dream shows that deep down, she remembers her original cat family.

Chi's Sweet Home (Vol. 3)
(Chi's Sweet Home series)
By Konami Kanata. Illus. by the author. Vertical, 2010. 144p. Ages 8-12

The stress of keeping a cat begins to affect everyone: a young friend visits and is too rough with Chi, and it's hard to keep a kitten secret from the landlady, especially when it becomes clear that there is at least one other cat around causing trouble. The grown-ups call him the "bear-cat," but Chi begins to like him and follow him around, calling him "Blackie." This volume closes on a hopeful note, with the family noticing a billboard advertising an apartment building that allows pets.

Chi's Sweet Home (Vol. 4)
(Chi's Sweet Home series)

By Konami Kanata. Illus. by the author. Vertical, 2010. 144p. Ages 8-12

The Yamadas have finally found a new apartment, one that allows pets. They won't have to avoid the landlady anymore, but all of them, especially Chi, need to get used to their new surroundings. Chi learns how to climb up stairs (but isn't sure how to climb down) and for the first time is allowed out in a yard, where she meets a new neighbor—a dog.

Chi's Sweet Home (Vol. 5)
(Chi's Sweet Home series)

By Konami Kanata. Illus. by the author. Vertical, 2011. 144p. Ages 8-12

Chi's beginning to venture farther afield and visits a playground, where another cat recognizes her but can't remember why (alert readers will understand Chi's cat family remains in the neighborhood). This cat tries to lead Chi back to her "mama," but Chi's not sure what a "mama" is and is a little scared. Fortunately, Chi is reunited with her friend Blackie, the large black cat from her former apartment building who caused so much trouble for the landlady.

Chi's Sweet Home (Vol. 6)
(Chi's Sweet Home series)

By Konami Kanata. Illus. by the author. Vertical, 2011. 144p. Ages 8-12

As Chi gets even more active and curious, the family is beginning to realize they need to watch out for her: she tries to touch a hot iron and is chided by Mommy. She chews a potentially poisonous house plant and is chided by Daddy. To Chi, Mommy and Daddy are "hogging" the items, and Chi relishes her time outside, free to roam in the yard and to the playground, where she finds another cat about her size to play with. Daddy brings home a collar with a bell for Chi to wear, and readers who can infer will sense the conflict to come when the family says, "Any way you look at her, she's a cute housecat now."

Chi's Sweet Home (Vol. 7)
(Chi's Sweet Home series)

By Konami Kanata. Illus. by the author. Vertical, 2011. 144p. Ages 8-12

Chi has scooted out the evening before and has spent her first night in the playground; at first, the family doesn't realize she hasn't slept inside. Later, during a visit to the playground, Chi gets separated from Yohei and Mommy and runs into her young cat friend, Cocchi. For the first time, it's explicit that Cocchi doesn't have a home and lives in the park. Chi keeps wondering where Cocchi's "home" is, and Cocchi doesn't know what to say. Blackie helps lead her home and shows Cocchi where Chi lives; Chi ends up having to go to the vet after eating something rotten outside; she isn't street smart like Cocchi and Blackie.

Chi's Sweet Home (Vol. 8)
(Chi's Sweet Home series)

By Konami Kanata. Illus. by the author. Vertical, 2012. 144p. Ages 8-12

Chi's and Cocchi's friendship begins to take off in the eighth volume; much of the focus is on the two young kittens playing and getting to know one another even better. It all happens outside; Chi's becoming less of a house cat and more of an outdoor cat, although she still relishes the ability to return to her comfortable home at night. Chi's exploring her own identity too, denying to Cocchi that she is a cat and insisting, "Chi is like Mommy, Daddy and Yohey [sic]." Unfortunately, Chi's eye gets irritated during one of her outdoor adventures, and by the end of this installment, she is relegated to wearing every pet's worst nightmare: the protective cone around the head.

Chi's Sweet Home (Vol. 9)
(Chi's Sweet Home series)

By Konami Kanata. Illus. by the author. Vertical, 2012. 144p. Ages 8-12

The tension between Chi's desire to go out and the family's desire to keep her a house cat finally comes to a head, when Chi is heartbroken at not being able to meet Cocchi in the park. Daddy comes up with what he thinks is a good solution: a leash for Chi! But when Chi escapes, she learns from Cocchi just what life as a stray is like. Happily, the family comes looking for Chi, finds the two kittens, and then it's Chi's turn to show Cocchi what living in a home is like.

Cross Game

By Mitsuru Adachi. Illus. by the author. VIZ Media, 2011. 576p. Ages 11-14

Ko and Wakaba have been close since childhood, much to the disgust of Wakaba's little sister Aoba. When Wakaba dies, both Ko and Aoba turn to baseball, Ko in an effort to live up to Wakaba's dream of him becoming a baseball star and Aoba as a way of coping with the loss of her sister. This sports manga progresses slowly, spending as much time developing characters as it does on game play. For these characters, sport is meaningful, but it isn't everything, which makes this slice-of-life drama accessible to jocks and nonjocks alike.

Drama

By Raina Telgemeier. Illus. by the author. Scholastic/Graphix, 2012. 240p. (DC) Ages 10-14

Callie, a middle school student, loves theater and adores her role as the set designer on the school's upcoming musical. Yet middle school life is an emotional roller coaster, and Callie is challenged by spats with her friends as well as her talent for picking the wrong boys as crushes. Fortunately, Callie makes a couple of new friends—identical twin boys, one of whom is openly gay—who help keep her sane and also add some much-needed talent to the show. The colorful, simple artwork brings the scenes to life.

Friends with Boys

By Faith Erin Hicks. Illus. by the author. First Second, 2012. 224p. Ages 12-14

Not only does Maggie have to handle her first year in high school after being homeschooled, she has to do it without the help of her older brothers, deal with difficult changes at home, make new friends, and figure out what to do with a neighborhood ghost that just won't leave her alone. Wonderfully expressive artwork does much of the heavy lifting in this story that will ring true with middle schoolers coping with change and preparing for the transition to high school.

Ghostopolis

By Doug TenNapel. Illus. by the author. Scholastic/Graphix, 2010. 288p. Ages 11-14

As an officer for the Supernatural Immigration Task Force, Frank Gallows catches ghosts on Earth and sends them back to the afterlife. However, during a troublesome deportation, he accidentally sends back Garth Hale, a boy who's terminally ill. Frank, with the help of his ex-fiancée (who's also a ghost), crosses over to the afterlife to try to rescue Garth. Meanwhile, Garth discovers that he has powers the ghosts don't have and is pursued by the evil ruler of Ghostopolis, who wants to use Garth's abilities to dominate his kingdom. Garth befriends a skeleton horse that he names Skinny and meets up with his grandfather, Cecil, who in the afterlife is Garth's age. The two team up to fight the evil ruler of Ghostopolis and get Garth home.

Giants Beware!

By Jorge Aguirre. Illus. by Rafael Rosado. First Second, 2012. 208p. Ages 7-10

This adventure starts out feeling familiar, but it turns out Claudette, her friend Marie, and her brother Gaston actually need to *save* the giant they'd set out to defeat. Themes of friendship, courage, and discovery have universal appeal and are presented in a fresh format here.

Guinea PIG, Pet Shop Private Eye: Fish You Were Here
(Guinea PIG, Pet Shop Private Eye series)

By Colleen AF Venable. Illus. by Stephanie Yue. Lerner/Graphic Universe, 2011. 48p. Ages 5-8

The animals for sale at Mr. Venezi's pet shop are thrilled at first with his new assistant Viola, who seems to know all about what each one of them needs. Mr. V. agrees and leaves her in charge, but it soon becomes clear she'd rather slack off than care for the pets. When it doesn't appear that Mr. V. is ever coming back, pet detective Sasspants the guinea pig and junior detective Hamisher the hamster swing into action. Silly Mr. V. is comically dim, as are the fish, who all seem to be named "Steve." But it all works out in the end once Mr. V. gets over his inferiority complex and Viola has a bit of a scare when she isn't paying attention on the job. Back matter includes information about fish, including the new one with a "pretty voice" (a pleco brought in by Viola).

Guinea PIG, Pet Shop Private Eye: The Ferret's a Foot
(Guinea PIG, Pet Shop Private Eye series)

By Colleen AF Venable. Illus. by Stephanie Yue. Lerner/Graphic Universe, 2011. 48p. Ages 5-8

Sasspants, the guinea pig sleuth, and Hamisher, the hamster sidekick, return to solve more crimes. This time, Sasspants and Hamisher must discover who is changing the signs on the pet store's cages before Hamisher falsely accuses the most obvious suspects. Is it the ferrets? They're the newest residents of the shop, and their signs don't seem to get defaced.

Expressive drawings and dry wit inspire giggles throughout all the stories in this series. Back matter includes information on mystery genre conventions, ferrets and goldfish, and animal-related professions; fans won't want to miss *Fish You Were Here* (2011).

Hereville: How Mirka Got Her Sword
(Hereville series)

By Barry Deutsch. Illus. by the author. Abrams/Amulet, 2010. 144p. Ages 9-12

Mirka, described as "yet another troll-fighting 11-year-old Orthodox Jewish girl," is full of energy and enthusiasm. Unfortunately, that enthusiasm is not for the things her stepmother, sister, or brother would like (knitting, husbands, and not getting into trouble, respectively). What Mirka does want is to fight dragons! But to do that, she'll need a sword, and she'll have to earn it the hard way. This original mix of folklore and fantasy blends genres and styles in a graphic novel format, continued in *Hereville: How Mirka Met a Meteorite* (2012).

Hereville: How Mirka Met a Meteorite
(Hereville series)

By Barry Deutsch. Illus. by the author. Abrams/Amulet, 2012. 128p. Ages 9-12

Mirka returns from her adventures in *How Mirka Got Her Sword* (2010), and this time she battles an unlikely foe: a meteorite that has morphed into a Mirka impostor and does all the things Mirka's family wishes she would do, including earning top grades. Mirka must learn to cope with Metty the meteorite and learns a bit more about Metty's backstory.

Johnny Boo and the Mean Little Boy
(Johnny Boo series)

By James Kochalka. Illus. by the author. Top Shelf, 2010. 40p. Ages 5-8

Johnny Boo isn't in the mood to play, telling his pet ghost Squiggle to go play with his other friends. Except Squiggle doesn't have any other friends. So when he's mistaken for a butterfly and captured in a little boy's net, Squiggle tries to make the best of it by turning the experience into a game and the mean little boy into his new friend. Consistent with the other books in this series, Kochalka's art is as charming as the story. The gentle (and slightly gross) humor will appeal to new readers and tickle the funny bones of fans of silly stories.

The Last Dragon

By Jane Yolen. Illus. by Rebecca Guay. Dark Horse, 2011. 144p. Ages 11-14

Two hundred years since the last dragon was thought to have been killed, the citizens panic when a new dragon hatches and begins to hunt. The townsfolk hire a "hero" to save them: a fast-talking young man with more skill at flying a kite than at wielding a sword. But it's Tansy, the healer's daughter, who knows the secret properties of the herb Dragons Bane and has the imagination to put the plant and the kite-flying together. This classic fairy tale is as eloquently told as it is beautifully illustrated; perfect for tweens who like their adventure with a dash of romance.

Maximum Ride: The Manga (Vol. 3)
(Maximum Ride: The Manga series)

By James Patterson and NaRae Lee. Illus. by NaRae Lee. Yen, 2010. 240p. Ages 10-14

In this adaptation of the popular fantasy and adventure series, readers share the thrill with Max and her family as they learn more about who they are, where they come from, and why they were "created." This installment follows "the flock" as they begin the search for their birth parents and find pleasure in a safe home, however temporary it might be. The graphic editions follow the novels faithfully. Text is abridged but effective, and the highly stylized illustrations draw out each character, adding to the emotional pull and excitement of the storyline. Volumes 4–5 (2011) and volume 6 (2012) continue the saga.

Maximum Ride: The Manga (Vol. 4)
(Maximum Ride: The Manga series)

By James Patterson and NaRae Lee. Illus. by NaRae Lee. Yen, 2011. 224p. Ages 10-14

The volumes in the Maximum Ride: The Manga series don't exactly parallel those in the text editions (e.g., vols. 4–5 span the content from *School's Out—Forever*, 2006), but fans of the story arc won't mind. In volume 4, Maximum Ride ("Max") knows she and the Flock can't stay for long in FBI agent Anne's house, where they've grown comfortable, but they all long to have their first real Thanksgiving dinner there. Unfortunately, their new school, which seems safe, isn't necessarily so.

Maximum Ride: The Manga (Vol. 5)
(Maximum Ride: The Manga series)

By James Patterson and NaRae Lee. Illus. by NaRae Lee. Yen, 2011. 240p. Ages 10-14

Tension between Max and the Flock increases as the group longs for the chance to drop its guard for once after escaping from the evil corporation ITEX's plan. Max's ambitions remain, however. The plot in volume 5 is closely linked to that in volume 4 (2011).

Maximum Ride: The Manga (Vol. 6)
(Maximum Ride: The Manga series)

By James Patterson and NaRae Lee. Illus. by NaRae Lee. Yen, 2012. 240p. Ages 10-14

Familiar elements from many literary dystopias (and, sadly, actual human history as well) surface again here as the Flock discovers their original function: to derail a plot to create a scientifically engineered master race and destroy all others. Unfortunately, it's going to be harder than ever now that they are separated and must each work independently to achieve their common goal.

Meanwhile: Pick Any Path

By Jason Shiga. Illus. by the author. Abrams/Amulet, 2010. 80p. Ages 8-14

First, Jimmy only has to decide between chocolate and vanilla ice cream. But when the neighborhood mad scientist invites Jimmy to try out three of his inventions, Jimmy begins a Choose Your Own Adventure–style journey that travels from the ordinary to the truly apocalyptic. Author Shiga uses the graphic novel format in ingenious ways to move the reader not only left to right between the panels, but from top to bottom and back and forth between pages via tubes and page tabs, creating a clever puzzle that will engage readers and maybe even teach them something about quantum physics.

Missile Mouse: The Star Crusher

By Jake Parker. Illus. by the author. Scholastic/Graphix, 2010. 176p. Ages 8-12

The brashly confident Missile Mouse is a secret agent at the Galactic Security Agency. When a top scientist is captured by enemy spies from the Rogue Imperium of Planets (a.k.a. RIP), Missile Mouse is assigned to rescue him, albeit with a new partner who's supposed to dampen MM's maverick tendencies. The mission is crucial since the apprehended scientist holds the key to the Star Crusher, a deadly weapon of mass destruction that RIP could use to take over the world. The fast-paced sci-fi text and illustrations, filled with action and humor, will have readers racing through the pages.

Nathan Hale's Hazardous Tales: Big Bad Ironclad!
(Nathan Hale's Hazardous Tales series)
By Nathan Hale. Illus. by the author. Abrams/Amulet, 2012. 128p. Ages 8-12

The truth can be stranger than fiction, and that's certainly the case here in this seemingly incredible account of ships made of iron and powered by steam that were created and utilized during the U. S. Civil War. History is brought to life in immediate fashion for contemporary readers via the graphic format, and back matter provides additional information and context.

Nathan Hale's Hazardous Tales: One Dead Spy
(Nathan Hale's Hazardous Tales series)
By Nathan Hale. Illus. by the author. Abrams/Amulet, 2012. 128p. Ages 8-12

Having been swallowed by a giant history book and had his brain filled with hundreds of facts about future American history, Nathan Hale promises to keep telling his hangman and executioner stories if they'll put off putting him to death. This crazy premise leads to a remarkably well-researched and engaging story of Hale's real-life experiences during the Revolutionary War. Back matter recaps the historical figures discussed in the book and answers questions about events that were not covered in the story. Using clever artwork, mnemonic devices, and lots of humor, contemporary Nathan Hale's series will have readers clamoring for more history, some of which can be found in *Big Bad Ironclad!* (2012).

The Odyssey
By Gareth Hinds. Illus. by the author. Candlewick, 2010. 256p. Ages 11-14

Odysseus's arduous and fantastic journey takes on a vivid life in this graphic narrative adaptation. Luscious watercolor illustrations rendered in vibrant green and blue hues and muted earth tones capture the volatility of the seascape and the hero's tenacity. Hinds's retelling in slightly adorned prose, highlighting Odysseus's breathtaking actions and deeply human emotions, maintains the story's timelessness and effortlessly carries the readers from one adventure to the next until the climatic end.

Olympians: Athena: Grey-Eyed Goddess
(Olympians series)

By George O'Connor. Illus. by the author. First Second, 2010. 80p. Ages 8-14

In the second book in the Olympians series, following *Zeus: King of the Gods* (2010), the Fates spin five tales about the goddess Athena, including stories of how she sprang fully grown from her father's forehead, how she came to adopt the name Pallas, and of her weaving competition with Arachne.

Olympians: Hades: Lord of the Dead
(Olympians series)

By George O'Connor. Illus. by the author. First Second, 2012. 80p. Ages 8-14

First, readers take a tour of the Underworld, as if they themselves have died. Later, more about Hades and his story unfold, including his abduction of Persephone, daughter of Zeus and Demeter. In this retelling, Persephone isn't an entirely unwilling abductee, fighting with her mother as any teen might. Contemporary language along with vibrant graphic illustrations bring the ancient myths alive for today's readers.

Olympians: Hera: The Goddess and Her Glory
(Olympians series)

By George O'Connor. Illus. by the author. First Second, 2011. 80p. Ages 8-14

Hera has a bad reputation, and why not? Among other undertakings as Zeus's bitter wife, she sets Heracles (better known nowadays by his Roman name, Hercules), Zeus's illegitimate son, a set of seemingly impossible tasks that he masters to become a powerful god in his own right. Here, Hera's story is explored a bit further, and a more nuanced picture of her emerges.

Olympians: Zeus: King of the Gods
(Olympians series)

By George O'Connor. Illus. by the author. First Second, 2010. 80p. Ages 8-14

Meticulously researched and drawn with a superhero sensibility, the stories in this series bring ancient Greek myths to life with an abundance of action, adventure, and just the right amount of modern language to keep the action flowing for modern kids. More fateful tales follow in *Athena: Grey-Eyed Goddess* (2010), *Hera: The Goddess and Her Glory* (2011), and *Hades: Lord of the Dead* (2012).

Princeless: Save Yourself

By Jeremy Whitley. Illus. by Mia Goodwin. Action Lab Entertainment, 2012. 116p. Ages 10-14

Princess Adrienne, whose father holds traditional beliefs about the respective roles of princes and princesses and has locked her in a tower, decides to take charge. Tired of waiting for a prince to come, she befriends her dragon protector and rescues herself, thank you very much. Gender stereotypes are turned on their heads in this high-energy fractured fairy tale, which is also refreshing in that the main cast includes people of color.

Sidekicks

By Dan Santat. Illus. by the author. Scholastic/Arthur A. Levine, 2011. 224p. Ages 8-11

Aging superhero Captain Amazing recognizes it's time for him to recruit a sidekick who will be able to take over when he retires. His pets, who compete for the job, each seem to possess a superpower: Manny, a.k.a. "Static Cat," can electrocute his opponents; Roscoe, a.k.a. "Metal Mutt," is able to generate a protective metal shell. Even tiny Shifty, the chameleon, can change color. Only Fluffy the hamster doesn't seem to have a power—that is, until Captain Amazing's team battles the evil Dr. Havoc. The group bickers like any other family, which makes their reconciliation even sweeter, in this action-adventure that also touches on themes of friendship and loyalty.

Smile

By Raina Telgemeier. Illus. by the author. Scholastic/Graphix, 2010. 224p. Ages 10-13

Raina knows that "something happens when you smile at people," but smiling isn't always easy as she negotiates the confusing world of friends, boys, and school from sixth grade through her sophomore year. Things get even more complicated as she endures endless rounds of oral surgery, retainers, and braces to repair major tooth damage. The spirited resilience that Raina shows through the roller coaster ride of her early teenage years makes her a highly appealing character. Expressive full-color artwork captures the awkward moments, the humor, and the occasional triumphs of growing up in this engaging graphic novel memoir.

Three Thieves: The Captive Prince
(Three Thieves series)

By Scott Chantler. Illus. by the author. Kids Can, 2012. 116p. Ages 8-10

Elements of romance enter into Dessa's saga for the first time when she rescues a kidnapped prince who subsequently falls in love with her. As in the two previous volumes, the combination of a strong female main character, bright and graphic illustrations, and a fast-paced plot keep interest high.

Three Thieves: The Sign of the Black Rock
(Three Thieves series)

By Scott Chantler. Illus. by the author. Kids Can, 2011. 112p. Ages 8-10

Dessa's adventures continue, and this time she's holed up for the night at a bit of a shady tavern while trying to evade the Queen's army and continue her quest for her brother. Also at the tavern are some of these soldiers, complicating matters. The suspense is leavened with some slapstick humor.

Three Thieves: Tower of Treasure
(Three Thieves series)

By Scott Chantler. Illus. by the author. Kids Can, 2010. 112p. Ages 8-10

Fourteen-year-old orphan Dessa has joined a traveling circus as a way of earning money while searching for her missing twin brother. When Dessa accidentally causes the day's earnings to be lost, she joins the circus's juggler and strongman in an attempt to rob the royal treasury. What results is the start of an adventure that carries into the next book in the series. Chantler's art is clear and bold, and his storytelling is easy to follow, with flashbacks shown in grays and sepia tones. The introduction of social issues will give fantasy and adventure fans something extra to chew on, here and in the following two series entries: *The Sign of the Black Rock* (2011) and *The Captive Prince* (2012).

Trickster: Native American Tales: A Graphic Collection

By Matt Dembicki (ed.). Illus. by various artists. Fulcrum, 2010. 232p. (DC) Ages 10-14

The trickster character is found in many cultures, from clever Raven of the Pacific Northwest, to Hershel of Ostropol, and Bre'r Rabbit. The trickster is often smart, sneaky, and prone to thievery. This remarkable anthology features trickster tales from tribal storytellers and writers across the country. Selections are authentic and unique, told with each teller's cultural sensibility, and each has a different illustrator. This diverse and compelling collection is both entertaining and thought provoking, exposing readers to cultures with which they may have little or no familiarity.

Twin Spica
(Twin Spica series)

By Kou Yaginuma. Illus. by the author. Vertical, 2010. 192p. Ages 11-14

For as long as she can remember, thirteen-year-old Asumi has dreamed of joining Japan's space program. But her diminutive size and family history all work against her as she struggles to gain entry into Tokyo's elite space school. But with the help of her classmates and the mysterious Mr. Lion, Asumi continues to beat the odds. A powerhouse of emotion fuels this story as it explores the motives and ambitions of its characters. Encourage boys to look past the girlish covers. Once they do, they'll be clamoring for the rest of the volumes in this series.

The Unsinkable Walker Bean

By Aaron Renier. Illus. by the author. First Second, 2010. 208p. Ages 8-10

When his grandfather, an admiral in a colonial-era navy, falls ill after discovering a mysterious pearl skull, Walker Bean stows away on a pirate ship in an attempt to return it to the ocean trench and to the sea witches from which it was stolen. The adventure begins on the first page, when Walker first hears the story of the witches, and rapidly unfolds, hitting expected pirate story tropes and inventing new ones as Walker races to save his grandfather. The fantastically detailed art features lush full-page spreads that readers will want to examine closely in order to not miss any jokes or clues.

A Wrinkle in Time: The Graphic Novel

By Madeleine L'Engle and Hope Larson. Illus. by Hope Larson. Farrar, 2012. 392p. Ages 10-14

This first-ever graphic retelling of the classic 1963 Newbery Medal winner offers readers a fresh look at this longtime favorite, on the occasion of the fiftieth anniversary of its publication. Subtle use of blues highlights the mostly black-and-white illustrations, still leaving much to the imagination. Skillful adaptation of the text retains the heart of the original story, capturing both the emotional pull and scientific flavor of L'Engle's writing. Graphic novel fans as well as devotees of the original will appreciate this version.

Yotsuba&! (Vol. 8)
(Yotsuba&! series)

By Azum Kiyohiko. Illus. by the author. Yen, 2010. 224p. Ages 8-14

Yotsuba "can find happiness in anything," and boy, does she. In this manga series still ongoing in Japan, Yotsuba attends a school festival and plays the kid-favorite (and adult nonfavorite) game of "opposite day." The interplay of reality (Yotsuba's story focuses on quotidian life rather than action-packed plot) and fantasy (Yotsuba may not be fully earthly) works surprisingly well. Full of charm and laugh-out-loud sight gags, the short chapters spotlight the sweetness found in everyday moments. The series, which began in 2009, continues with volume 9 (2010), volume 10 (2011), and volume 11 (2012).

Yotsuba&! (Vol. 9)
(Yotsuba&! series)

By Azum Kiyohiko. Illus. by the author. Yen, 2010. 224p. Ages 8-14

Exuberant Yotsuba needs a schedule to remind her of all things she needs to do in a day (such as use the bathroom) amid all the things she wants to do. Even reading about her busy, busy day may feel tiring to an adult but not to her high-energy young fans.

Yotsuba&! (Vol. 10)
(Yotsuba&! series)

By Azum Kiyohiko. Illus. by the author. Yen, 2011. 224p. Ages 8-14

Adults who play games with young children will be familiar with the rapid pace of rules changes and the impatience that goes along with them. Playing hide-and-seek, tag, and more with Daddy, Yotsuba sometimes engineers things her own way, but sometimes "lets" him win too.

Yotsuba&! (Vol. 11)
(Yotsuba&! series)

By Azum Kiyohiko. Illus. by the author. Yen, 2012. 224p. Ages 8-14

Yotsuba's got a new camera and in trademark irrepressible style, she wants to photograph everyone she sees. She needs to learn a little bit about boundaries and feels a bit boundary challenged herself when her teddy bear has an encounter with a dog.

Zita the Spacegirl: Legends of Zita the Spacegirl
(Zita the Spacegirl series)

By Ben Hatke. Illus. by the author. First Second, 2012. 224p. Ages 8-12

Zita follows her heroics from *Zita the Spacegirl* (2011) by going on an interplanetary victory tour. But her adventures aren't over; now that she's famous, a robotic impostor surfaces, and she must hijack a spaceship and learn to work with the "Imprint-O-Tron" to save yet another planet.

Zita the Spacegirl: Zita the Spacegirl
(Zita the Spacegirl series)

By Ben Hatke. Illus. by the author. First Second, 2011. 188p. Ages 8-12

Zita lives a normal life, going to school and playing with her friend Joseph. Normal, that is, until Zita finds a strange object in her backyard and watches Joseph get pulled through it into another world. Zita does the only thing she can and follows him. Zita must partner with the mysterious and untrustworthy Piper, his Giant Mouse, and a reformed Battle Orb named One in order to find and rescue Joseph and escape this strange world before it, and they, are destroyed by a giant asteroid. Vibrant artwork and an exciting dialogue keep the story moving and leave the reader eager for Zita's next adventure, *Legends of Zita the Spacegirl* (2012).

Poetry

Recommendations for cultivating a diverse collection are indicated by "(DC)."

Around the World on Eighty Legs

By Amy Gibson. Illus. by Daniel Salmieri. Scholastic, 2011. 56p. Ages 4-8

Fun illustrated poems focused on animals—some familiar, some less so—make this an instant favorite. Nonfiction enthusiasts will appreciate the back matter, which includes factual data and a photograph of each animal included in the text. The poems work well as read-alouds for those not ready to read on their own, and the illustrations are energetic and accessible. A rough map identifies where each animal could be found in the wild. This overall kid-friendly package combines the best of entertainment and education.

Dark Emperor and Other Poems of the Night

By Joyce Sidman. Illus. by Rick Allen. Houghton Mifflin Harcourt, 2010. 32p. Ages 8-11

Thoughtfully packaged with endpapers that contribute to the story, this book takes readers on a trip through the woods from dusk until dawn. Each page turn introduces a new nocturnal being and features a rich portrait, poem, and just a taste of nonfiction information about the animal (or mushroom, as the case may be). The poetry is written in different styles and with a range of solemnity, but each subject is given space to shine. The linoleum-block print illustrations are bold and expressive; readers will be drawn into the dark and shown a world they may not know exists. NEWBERY HONOR BOOK

Forgive Me, I Meant to Do It: False Apology Poems

By Gail Carson Levine. Illus. by Matthew Cordell. HarperCollins, 2012. 80p. Ages 8-11

Inspired by the famous "This Is Just to Say" poem by William Carlos Williams, here is a new batch of funny "false apology poems" starring fairy tale characters, children's book figures, and plain old kids. For example, we learn why Humpty Dumpty fell ("all the king's horses / and all the king's men / were bored") and read a brother's unconvincing explanation of why he and the cat ate all his sister's ice cream. Readers who enjoy the sly humor and comical line drawings might just be inspired to come up with some apologetic poetry of their own.

I, Too, Am America

By Langston Hughes. Illus. by Bryan Collier. Simon & Schuster, 2012. 40p. (DC) Ages 5-9

Langston Hughes's classic poem is interpreted by intriguing collage art portraying Pullman porters, who worked long hours for steady pay and equality. Here, the porters collect up detritus—newspapers, jazz records—and fling it out the windows, where it is spread by the wind to other African Americans nationwide. The recurring stars-and-stripes visual theme reinforces the patriotism of people who had an unequal chance at the American dream. CORETTA SCOTT KING ILLUSTRATOR HONOR BOOK

Mirror, Mirror: A Book of Reversible Verse

By Marilyn Singer. Illus. by Josée Masse. Dutton, 2010. 32p. Ages 8-11

Paired poems retell fairy tales with surprising twists. Red Riding Hood and the wolf, for example, each tell one side of the story using the exact same lines but in reverse order! This inventive "reverso" poetry form is used to rework "Snow White," "Sleeping Beauty," and other familiar tales, injecting sly wit and double meanings. Imaginative paintings accompanying each pair of poems use split-page layouts to depict both contrasting viewpoints in one image. This brings a unique and original presentation that may inspire kids to try their own "reversos."

Muu, Moo! Rimas de animales / Animal Nursery Rhymes

By Alma Flor Ada. Illus. by Viví Escrivá. HarperCollins/Rayo, 2010. 48p. (DC) Ages 3-7

Sixteen nursery rhymes from a variety of Spanish-speaking cultures (Spain, Puerto Rico, Argentina, and more) are presented in Spanish alongside loose English translations meant to capture tone and feel rather than direct, literal, word-to-word meaning. Each has an animal at its heart, and they're all softly illustrated in soft pastel tones.

Snook Alone

By Marilyn Nelson. Illus. by Timothy Basil Ering. Candlewick, 2010. 48p. Ages 5-8

This exquisite portrait of the love between a man and his dog is characterized by an impeccably paced, poetic text and dramatic acrylic and ink illustrations. Snook, a "loyal rat terrier," and Abba Jacob, a monk, carry out their daily routines on an isolated island until one day they are separated by a storm and Snook must fend for himself. The heartbreaking, emotional story is leavened by their eventual joyful reunion.

Step Gently Out

By Helen Frost. Illus. by Rick Leider. Candlewick, 2012. 32p. Ages 4-7

Young children often seem to go constantly at a mile a minute; here, they're invited to slow down and consider the world from an insect's point of view. A collection of poems introduces what might be observed after stepping out gently: a cricket jumping, a spider spinning, and more, throughout the day and into night. Compelling close-up photographs in full color make creatures sometimes considered ugly, beautiful.

Swirl by Swirl: Spirals in Nature

By Joyce Sidman. Illus. by Beth Krommes. Houghton Mifflin Harcourt, 2011. 40p. Ages 4-10

The most beautiful things in nature are often the most overlooked; here, a poetic text and gorgeous artwork present the wonders of the many spirals found in the natural world. From sleeping woodchucks, to lady ferns uncoiling in the morning, to the horns of the merino sheep, the spare text and intricate scratchboard illustrations illuminate the soft, strong, graceful, bold, and beautiful spiral. Suitable for reading aloud to a group, this can also be enjoyed one-on-one or read solo.

UnBEElieveables: Honeybee Poems and Paintings

By Douglas Florian. Illus. by the author. Simon & Schuster/Beach Lane, 2012. 32p. Ages 7-10

There's no need to be afraid of the stings of these colorfully illustrated bees. Poetry and facts accompany child-friendly collage art to introduce the common garden insect. Information such as their life cycle, life in the hive, communication, and more is covered, and back matter includes lists of further reading and websites.

Walking on Earth and Touching the Sky: Poetry and Prose by Lakota Youth at Red Cloud Indian School

By Timothy P. McLaughlin (ed.). Illus. by S. D. Nelson. Abrams, 2012. 80p. (DC) Ages 12-14

This collection of poetry and prose written by students at Red Cloud Indian School on the Pine Ridge Indian Reservation in South Dakota offers an honest look at contemporary Native American life. Everyday experiences with the natural world and family living are included, as are harder-hitting sections on racism and the legacy of poverty and oppression this population has coped with.

Water Sings Blue: Ocean Poems

By Kate Coombs. Illus. by Meilo So. Chronicle, 2012. 32p. Ages 5-8

Twenty-three poems of varied styles and lengths (although none feels too long) focus on the wonder of the ocean and the things within and around it, both expected and not. Layouts and watercolor illustrations parallel the text's variety of perspectives and styles, although watery blue logically predominates and helps carry the tropical theme throughout. Poetry and art here celebrate the sunny seaside, all year round.

Won Ton: A Cat Tale Told in Haiku

By Lee Wardlaw. Illus. by Eugene Yelchin. Holt, 2011. 40p. Ages 4-8

Not exactly haiku, but a similar type of poetry called *senryu*, focuses on the adoption of a shelter cat. Simple, bold illustrations of the appealing gray kitty on clean backgrounds aptly capture the poems and the emotions expressed in them. Kids who don't think they like poetry will be pleasantly surprised here.

You Don't Even Know Me: Stories and Poems about Boys

By Sharon G. Flake. Disney/Jump at the Sun, 2010. 208p. Ages 12-14

These alternating poems and stories focus on boys—their dreams, their goals, their relationships, their problems, and their pain. From sixteen-year-old Tow-Kay, who marries his pregnant girlfriend; to James, who reveals his twin brother's secret; to Tyler, a player; and to Laron, who is infected with HIV; Flake presents a myriad of young African American lives that readers will get to know and remember.

Appendixes

Books by Age Level

Ages 0-3
Animal 1 2 3
Hey Diddle Diddle and Other Favorite Nursery Rhymes
Trains Go
Tubby

Ages 0-4
Clare Beaton's Farmyard Rhymes

Ages 0-5
A Kiss Means I Love You
Moonlight

Ages 1-3
Potty

Ages 1-4
Tuck Me In

Ages 1-6
Goodnight, Goodnight Construction Site

Ages 2-4
All Kinds of Kisses
Dinosaur vs. the Potty
Hippopposites

Ages 2-5
Bea at Ballet
Bear Has a Story to Tell
Blue Sky
Broom, Zoom!
Cat the Cat: Let's Say Hi to Friends Who Fly!
Cat the Cat: Time to Sleep, Sheep the Sheep!
Cat the Cat: What's Your Sound, Hound the Hound?
Cat the Cat: Who Is That?
Fiesta Babies
Green
Little White Rabbit
Oh, Daddy!
The Pout-Pout Fish in the Big-Big Dark
Shoe-la-la!
There's Going to Be a Baby
Tweak Tweak
Under Ground

Ages 2-6
A Sick Day for Amos McGee
Spot the Animals: A Lift-the-Flap Book of Colors

Ages 2-7
Squeak, Rumble, Whomp! Whomp! Whomp! A Sonic Adventure

Ages 2-8
All Things Bright and Beautiful

Ages 3-5
A Ball for Daisy
Do You Know Which Ones Will Grow?

Don't Want to Go!
The Duckling Gets a Cookie!?
I'm the Best
Little Mouse's Big Secret
Little Pig Joins the Band
A Long Piece of String
The Loud Book
Night Knight
The Quiet Book

Ages 3-6

The Baby That Roared
Backseat A-B-See
Blue Chicken
Boom Boom Go Away!
Dot
Eight Days Gone
Elephant & Piggie: Can I Play Too?
Elephant & Piggie: Happy Pig Day!
Elephant & Piggie: I Am Going!
Elephant & Piggie: I Broke My Trunk!
Elephant & Piggie: Let's Go for a Drive!
Elephant & Piggie: Listen to My Trumpet!
Elephant & Piggie: Should I Share My Ice Cream?
Elephant & Piggie: We Are in a Book!
Faster! Faster!
The Hueys in the New Sweater
The Human Body
I Can Help
I Know a Wee Piggy
It's a Tiger
Jo MacDonald Saw a Pond
LMNO Peas
Mini Racer
More Bears!
The Neighborhood Sing-Along
Pecan Pie Baby

Purple Little Bird
Rah, Rah, Radishes! A Vegetable Chant
The Red Hen
Red Knit Cap Girl
What's Special about Me, Mama?
Where's My T-R-U-C-K?
You're Finally Here!

Ages 3-7

A Beach Tail
Bring on the Birds
Edwin Speaks Up
Good News, Bad News
If You Give a Dog a Donut
Kite Day: A Bear and Mole Story
Knuffle Bunny Free: An Unexpected Diversion
Llama Llama: Llama Llama Holiday Drama
Llama Llama: Llama Llama Home with Mama
Llama Llama: Llama Llama Time to Share
Muu, Moo! Rimas de animales / Animal Nursery Rhymes
No Sleep for the Sheep!
Please Take Me for a Walk
Press Here
Solomon Crocodile
Toads on Toast
Where's Walrus?
Z Is for Moose

Ages 3-8

Beautiful Oops!
The Cazuela That the Farm Maiden Stirred
Homer
Nursery Rhyme Comics: 50 Timeless Rhymes from 50 Celebrated Cartoonists

Ages 4-6

Except If
Otto the Book Bear
Shark vs. Train
Sleep like a Tiger

Ages 4-7

1-2-3 Peas
And Then It's Spring
The Artist Who Painted a Blue Horse
Blackout
A Bus Called Heaven
Caveman: A B.C. Story
Creepy Carrots!
Dodsworth: Dodsworth in Rome
Extra Yarn
Goldilocks and the Three Dinosaurs
How to Be Friends with a Dragon
I Spy Under the Sea
I Want My Hat Back
Ice
I'm Bored
The Little Red Pen
Lottie Paris Lives Here
Monkey Colors
My Garden
Nighttime Ninja
Penny and Her Doll
Penny and Her Song
Spike the Mixed-Up Monster
Step Gently Out
Suppose You Meet a Dinosaur: A First Book of Manners
This Is Not My Hat
Tía Isa Wants a Car
When a Dragon Moves In
You Can Be a Friend

Ages 4-8

All the Water in the World

All the Way to America: The Story of a Big Italian Family and a Little Shovel

Another Brother

Around the World on Eighty Legs

Balloons over Broadway: The True Story of the Puppeteer of Macy's Parade

Bear in Love

C. R. Mudgeon

Chloe and the Lion

Chopsticks

The Christmas Coat

Dear Primo: A Letter to My Cousin

Dino-Baseball

E-mergency!

Farm

A Home for Bird

Hooray for Amanda & Her Alligator!

Interrupting Chicken

Marisol McDonald Doesn't Match / Marisol McDonald no combina

Me, Frida

Me . . . Jane

Monsieur Marceau: Actor without Words

One Cool Friend

Pete the Cat: I Love My White Shoes

Pete the Cat: Pete the Cat and His Four Groovy Buttons

Pete the Cat: Pete the Cat Saves Christmas

Puss in Boots

The Rabbit Problem

Ready, Set, 100th Day!

See Me Run

Shadow

Sky Color

Suryia and Roscoe: The True Story of an Unlikely Friendship

Three Little Pigs: An Architectural Tale

Underground

Village Garage
Who Built the Stable? A Nativity Poem
Won Ton: A Cat Tale Told in Haiku

Ages 4-10
Swirl by Swirl: Spirals in Nature

Ages 5-7
April and Esme, Tooth Fairies
Benny and Penny: Benny and Penny in Lights Out
Benny and Penny: Benny and Penny in the Toy Breaker
Bone Dog
Clever Jack Takes the Cake
Don't Squish the Sasquatch!
East Dragon, West Dragon
Henry's Heart: A Boy, His Heart, and a New Best Friend
How Many Jelly Beans? A Giant Book of Giant Numbers!
Little Black Crow
Looking at Lincoln
Meet the Dogs of Bedlam Farm
My Mom Has X-Ray Vision
Question Boy Meets Little Miss Know-It-All
Rabbit & Robot: The Sleepover
Three by the Sea
The Tooth Fairy Meets El Ratón Pérez

Ages 5-8
Abe Lincoln's Dream
Acoustic Rooster and His Barnyard Band
Animal Crackers Fly the Coop
Art & Max
Chalk
City Dog, Country Frog
The Cloud Spinner
Colorful Dreamer: The Story of Henri Matisse
Eight Days: A Story of Haiti
Family Pack

Goal!
Grandpa Green
Guinea PIG, Pet Shop Private Eye: Fish You Were Here
Guinea PIG, Pet Shop Private Eye: The Ferret's a Foot
How Did That Get in My Lunchbox? The Story of Food
I Have a Dream: Dr. Martin Luther King, Jr.
Johnny Boo and the Mean Little Boy
Ladder to the Moon
Laundry Day
Ling & Ting: Not Exactly the Same!
Little Treasures: Endearments from around the World
My Brother Charlie
Perfect Square
Snook Alone
Stink: Solar System Superhero
Summer Jackson: Grown Up
*Ten Rules You Absolutely Must Not Break If You Want to Survive the
    School Bus*
Water Sings Blue: Ocean Poems
Zig and Wikki in the Cow

Ages 5-9
Big Red Lollipop
Boot & Shoe
Can We Save the Tiger?
Chavela and the Magic Bubble
Coral Reefs
Diego Rivera: His World and Ours
I, Too, Am America
Island: A Story of the Galápagos
Nic Bishop Snakes
Oh, No!
Otis and the Tornado

Ages 5-10
Monkey: A Trickster Tale from India
Of Thee I Sing: A Letter to My Daughters

Ages 6-8
A Is for Musk Ox
Jack and the Beanstalk
Ocean Sunlight: How Tiny Plants Feed the Seas
The Quiet Place
*A Strange Place to Call Home: The World's Most Dangerous Habitats and
    the Animals That Call Them Home*
Super Diaper Baby 2: The Invasion of the Potty Snatchers
Wumbers: It's Words Cre8ted with Numbers

Ages 6-9
Auntie Yang's Great Soybean Picnic
Clara Lee and the Apple Pie Dream
It Jes' Happened: When Bill Traylor Started to Draw
Jangles: A Big Fish Story
Orangutans Are Ticklish: Fun Facts from an Animal Photographer

Ages 6-10
Actual Times: America Is Under Attack: The Day the Towers Fell
Bink & Gollie
Each Kindness
Lulu and the Brontosaurus
Sit-In: How Four Friends Stood Up by Sitting Down

Ages 6-12
100 Things You Should Know about Elephants

Ages 7-9
A Butterfly Is Patient
Saving Audie: A Pit Bull Puppy Gets a Second Chance

Ages 7-10
Annie and Helen
Bones: Skeletons and How They Work
Brother Sun, Sister Moon: Saint Francis of Assisi's Canticle of the Creatures
*Captain Underpants: Captain Underpants and the Terrifying Return of
    Tippy Tinkletrousers*

Clementine: Clementine, Friend of the Week
Clementine: Clementine and the Family Meeting
Electric Ben: The Amazing Life and Times of Benjamin Franklin
Giants Beware!
How to Clean a Hippopotamus: A Look at Unusual Animal Partnerships
Older than the Stars
Sugar Plum Ballerinas: Dancing Diva
Sugar Plum Ballerinas: Perfectly Prima
Sugar Plum Ballerinas: Sugar Plums to the Rescue!
Sugar Plum Ballerinas: Terrible Terrel
UnBEElieveables: Honeybee Poems and Paintings

Ages 7-11
Big Wig: A Little History of Hair
The Extraordinary Mark Twain (According to Susy)
A Nation's Hope

Ages 8-10
Babymouse: A Very Babymouse Christmas
Babymouse: Babymouse Burns Rubber
Babymouse: Babymouse for President
Babymouse: Cupcake Tycoon
Babymouse: Mad Scientist
Bake Sale
Dave the Potter: Artist, Poet, Slave
Dyamonde Daniel Books: Almost Zero
Dyamonde Daniel Books: Halfway to Perfect
J. J. Tully Mystery: The Trouble with Chickens
Three Thieves: The Captive Prince
Three Thieves: The Sign of the Black Rock
Three Thieves: Tower of Treasure
The Unsinkable Walker Bean

Ages 8-11
Dark Emperor and Other Poems of the Night
Forgive Me, I Meant to Do It: False Apology Poems
Henry Knox: Bookseller, Soldier, Patriot

Knights' Tales: The Adventures of Sir Balin the Ill-Fated
Knights' Tales: The Adventures of Sir Gawain the True
Liberty Porter, First Daughter: Cleared for Takeoff
Liberty Porter, First Daughter: Liberty Porter, First Daughter
Liberty Porter, First Daughter: New Girl in Town
Mirror, Mirror: A Book of Reversible Verse
Sidekicks
Starry River of the Sky
Thunder Birds: Nature's Flying Predators

Ages 8-12

The Beetle Book
Big Nate: In a Class By Himself
Bigfoot Boy: Into the Woods
The Cheshire Cheese Cat: A Dickens of a Tale
Chi's Sweet Home (Vol. 1)
Chi's Sweet Home (Vol. 2)
Chi's Sweet Home (Vol. 3)
Chi's Sweet Home (Vol. 4)
Chi's Sweet Home (Vol. 5)
Chi's Sweet Home (Vol. 6)
Chi's Sweet Home (Vol. 7)
Chi's Sweet Home (Vol. 8)
Chi's Sweet Home (Vol. 9)
Chuck Close: Face Book
Ellie McDoodle: Best Friends Fur-Ever
Ellie McDoodle: Most Valuable Player
The Familiars
The House Baba Built: An Artist's Childhood in China
Junonia
*Maximilian & the Mystery of the Guardian Angel: A Bilingual Lucha
    Libre Thriller*
Missile Mouse: The Star Crusher
The Mostly True Story of Jack
Nathan Hale's Hazardous Tales: Big Bad Ironclad!
Nathan Hale's Hazardous Tales: One Dead Spy
The One and Only Ivan

Secret: This Isn't What It Looks Like
Secret: You Have to Stop This
Turtle in Paradise
Who Could That Be at This Hour?
Who Was Rosa Parks?
Young Fredle
Zita the Spacegirl: Legends of Zita the Spacegirl
Zita the Spacegirl: Zita the Spacegirl

Ages 8-14

Meanwhile: Pick Any Path
Olympians: Athena: Grey-Eyed Goddess
Olympians: Hades: Lord of the Dead
Olympians: Hera: The Goddess and Her Glory
Olympians: Zeus: King of the Gods
Yotsuba&! (Vol. 8)
Yotsuba&! (Vol. 9)
Yotsuba&! (Vol. 10)
Yotsuba&! (Vol. 11)

Ages 9-11

The Adventures of Nanny Piggins
Amulet: The Last Council
Fake Mustache: How Jodie O'Rodeo and Her Wonder Horse (and Some Nerdy Kid) Saved the U.S. Presidential Election from a Mad Genius Criminal Mastermind
Griffin & Co. Adventures: Framed
Griffin & Co. Adventures: Showoff
One Crazy Summer
Origami Yoda: Darth Paper Strikes Back
Origami Yoda: The Secret of the Fortune Wookiee
Origami Yoda: The Strange Case of Origami Yoda
Secrets at Sea

Ages 9-12

90 Miles to Havana
Amelia Rules! Her Permanent Record
Amelia Rules! Superheroes

Amelia Rules! The Meaning of Life . . . and Other Stuff
Amelia Rules! The Tweenage Guide to Not Being Unpopular
Amelia Rules! The Whole World's Crazy
Amelia Rules! True Things (Adults Don't Want Kids to Know)
Amelia Rules! What Makes You Happy
Amelia Rules! When the Past Is a Present
Books of Beginning: The Emerald Atlas
Books of Beginning: The Fire Chronicle
The Candymakers
Charlie Joe Jackson: Charlie Joe Jackson's Guide to Extra Credit
Charlie Joe Jackson: Charlie Joe Jackson's Guide to Not Reading
Cosmic
Diary of a Wimpy Kid: Cabin Fever
Diary of a Wimpy Kid: The Third Wheel
Diary of a Wimpy Kid: The Ugly Truth
Falling In
The Grand Plan to Fix Everything
Heart and Soul: The Story of America and African Americans
Hereville: How Mirka Got Her Sword
Hereville: How Mirka Met a Meteorite
Liar & Spy
Mammoths and Mastodons: Titans of the Ice Age
The Mighty Miss Malone
My Life as a Stuntboy
Ninth Ward
Peter Nimble and His Fantastic Eyes
Popularity Papers: Research for the Social Improvement and General Betterment of Lydia Goldblatt & Julie Graham-Chang
Popularity Papers: The Long-Distance Dispatch between Lydia Goldblatt & Julie Graham-Chang
Popularity Papers: The Rocky Road Trip of Lydia Goldblatt & Julie Graham-Chang
Popularity Papers: Words of (Questionable) Wisdom from Lydia Goldblatt and Julie Graham-Chang
A Tale Dark and Grimm
The Trouble with May Amelia
Wonkenstein

Ages 9-13

Cardboard
Hand in Hand: Ten Black Men Who Changed America
Jimi: Sounds like a Rainbow
Liesl & Po
Mockingbird
Moon Over Manifest
Titanic: Voices from the Disaster
The Underdogs
Wonder
Wonderstruck

Ages 9-14

Three Times Lucky

Ages 10-12

Chickadee
Drawing from Memory
The False Prince
Winnie Years: Ten
Winnie Years: Thirteen plus One

Ages 10-13

Beyonders: A World without Heroes
Beyonders: Seeds of Rebellion
Breaking Stalin's Nose
Disasters: Natural and Man-Made Catastrophes through the Centuries
Heroes of Olympus: The Lost Hero
Heroes of Olympus: The Mark of Athena
Heroes of Olympus: The Son of Neptune
How They Croaked: The Awful Ends of the Awfully Famous
Kane Chronicles: The Red Pyramid
Kane Chronicles: The Serpent's Shadow
Kane Chronicles: The Throne of Fire
Keeper
Out of My Mind
Ranger's Apprentice: Erak's Ransom

Ranger's Apprentice: Halt's Peril
Ranger's Apprentice: The Emperor of Nihon-Ja
Ranger's Apprentice: The Kings of Clonmel
Ranger's Apprentice: The Lost Stories
The Ring of Solomon
Scumble
Smile
Ungifted
Warriors: Omen of the Stars: Night Whispers
Warriors: Omen of the Stars: Sign of the Moon
We Could Be Brothers
The Wimpy Kid Movie Diary: How Greg Heffley Went Hollywood
The Wonder of Charlie Anne
Zora and Me

Ages 10-14

Abraham Lincoln & Frederick Douglass: The Story behind an American Friendship
Amelia Lost: The Life and Disappearance of Amelia Earhart
The Batboy
Bluefish
Bomb: The Race to Build—and Steal—the World's Most Dangerous Weapon
Broxo
Chronicles of Egg: Deadweather and Sunrise
Drama
The Dreamer
The Girl Who Circumnavigated Fairyland in a Ship of Her Own Making
The Good, the Bad, and the Barbie: A Doll's History and Her Impact on Us
Heart of a Samurai
The Impossible Rescue: The True Story of an Amazing Arctic Adventure
Inside Out and Back Again
Maximum Ride: The Manga (Vol. 3)
Maximum Ride: The Manga (Vol. 4)
Maximum Ride: The Manga (Vol. 5)
Maximum Ride: The Manga (Vol. 6)

A Monster Calls
Moonbird: A Year on the Wind with the Great Survivor B95
*The Notorious Benedict Arnold: A True Story of Adventure, Heroism, &
    Treachery*
Okay for Now
Princeless: Save Yourself
*Saga of the Sioux: An Adaptation of Dee Brown's Bury My Heart at
    Wounded Knee*
Sidekicks
*Treasury of Greek Mythology: Classic Stories of Gods, Goddesses, Heroes
    & Monsters*
Trickster: Native American Tales: A Graphic Collection
Western Mysteries: The Case of the Deadly Desperados
What's New, Cupcake? Ingeniously Simple Designs for Every Occasion
A Wrinkle in Time: The Graphic Novel

Ages 11-13
A Long Walk to Water: Based on a True Story

Ages 11-14
Amulet: Prince of the Elves
Amulet: The Cloud Searchers
Around the World
Bad Island
The Big Adventures of Majoko (Vol. 3)
The Big Adventures of Majoko (Vol. 4)
The Big Adventures of Majoko (Vol. 5)
Countdown
Cross Game
The Dead
Ghostopolis
Hidden
The Last Dragon
Legend
Mockingjay
The Odyssey
Ship Breaker
Twin Spica

Ages 12-14

Anya's Ghost
As Easy as Falling Off the Face of the Earth
Beauty Queens
Between Shades of Gray
Cinder
Clockwork Angel
Daughter of Smoke and Bone
Don't Call Me Hero
Friends with Boys
Hurricane Dancers: The First Caribbean Pirate Shipwreck
Inheritance
Long Lankin
My Sister Lives on the Mantelpiece
On the Day I Died
Son
Trash
*Walking on Earth and Touching the Sky: Poetry and Prose by Lakota
    Youth at Red Cloud Indian School*
You Don't Even Know Me: Stories and Poems about Boys

Ages 13-14

Bitterblue
Bootleg: Murder, Moonshine, and the Lawless Years of Prohibition
The Scorpio Races
So For Real: Cool like That

Books by Genre/Subject

Alphabet
A Is for Musk Ox
Backseat A-B-See
Caveman: A B.C. Story
E-mergency!
LMNO Peas
Z Is for Moose

Animals
100 Things You Should Know about Elephants
The Beetle Book
Bring on the Birds
A Butterfly Is Patient
Can We Save the Tiger?
Mammoths and Mastodons: Titans of the Ice Age
Moonbird: A Year on the Wind with the Great Survivor B95
Nic Bishop Snakes
Orangutans Are Ticklish: Fun Facts from an Animal Photographer
Spot the Animals: A Lift-the-Flap Book of Colors
Suryia and Roscoe: The True Story of an Unlikely Friendship
UnBEElieveables: Honeybee Poems and Paintings

Art

Art & Max
The Artist Who Painted a Blue Horse

Autobiography/ Memoir

All the Way to America: The Story of a Big Italian Family and a Little Shovel
Chuck Close: Face Book
Drawing from Memory
The House Baba Built: An Artist's Childhood in China

Biography

Abe Lincoln's Dream
Abraham Lincoln & Frederick Douglass: The Story behind an American Friendship
Amelia Lost: The Life and Disappearance of Amelia Earhart
Annie and Helen
Balloons over Broadway: The True Story of the Puppeteer of Macy's Parade
Colorful Dreamer: The Story of Henri Matisse
Dave the Potter: Artist, Poet, Slave
Diego Rivera: His World and Ours
Electric Ben: The Amazing Life and Times of Benjamin Franklin
Hand in Hand: Ten Black Men Who Changed America
Henry Knox: Bookseller, Soldier, Patriot
I Have a Dream: Dr. Martin Luther King, Jr.
It Jes' Happened: When Bill Traylor Started to Draw
Jimi: Sounds like a Rainbow
Me, Frida
Me . . . Jane
Monsieur Marceau: Actor without Words
A Nation's Hope
The Notorious Benedict Arnold: A True Story of Adventure, Heroism, & Treachery
Who Was Rosa Parks?

Classic
The Odyssey

Cookbook
What's New, Cupcake? Ingeniously Simple Designs for Every Occasion

Counting
1-2-3 Peas
Animal 1 2 3

Current Events
Actual Times: America Is Under Attack: The Day the Towers Fell

Dystopia
Mockingjay
Ship Breaker

Ecology
Can We Save the Tiger?
Island: A Story of the Galápagos
Moonbird: A Year on the Wind with the Great Survivor B95
Ocean Sunlight: How Tiny Plants Feed the Seas

Family
Another Brother

Fantasy
Amulet: Prince of the Elves
Amulet: The Cloud Searchers
Amulet: The Last Council
Beyonders: A World without Heroes
Beyonders: Seeds of Rebellion
The Big Adventures of Majoko (Vol. 3)
The Big Adventures of Majoko (Vol. 4)
The Big Adventures of Majoko (Vol. 5)
Bigfoot Boy: Into the Woods
Bitterblue

Books of Beginning: The Emerald Atlas
Books of Beginning: The Fire Chronicle
Broxo
Cardboard
Chronicles of Egg: Deadweather and Sunrise
Cinder
Clockwork Angel
Daughter of Smoke and Bone
Falling In
The False Prince
The Familiars
Ghostopolis
Giants Beware!
The Girl Who Circumnavigated Fairyland in a Ship of Her Own Making
Hereville: How Mirka Got Her Sword
Hereville: How Mirka Met a Meteorite
Heroes of Olympus: The Lost Hero
Heroes of Olympus: The Mark of Athena
Heroes of Olympus: The Son of Neptune
Inheritance
Kane Chronicles: The Red Pyramid
Kane Chronicles: The Serpent's Shadow
Kane Chronicles: The Throne of Fire
Knights' Tales: The Adventures of Sir Balin the Ill-Fated
Knights' Tales: The Adventures of Sir Gawain the True
The Last Dragon
Liesl & Po
Long Lankin
Maximum Ride: The Manga (Vol. 3)
Maximum Ride: The Manga (Vol. 4)
Maximum Ride: The Manga (Vol. 5)
Maximum Ride: The Manga (Vol. 6)
Missile Mouse: The Star Crusher
The Mostly True Story of Jack
Peter Nimble and His Fantastic Eyes
Ranger's Apprentice: Erak's Ransom
Ranger's Apprentice: Halt's Peril

Ranger's Apprentice: The Emperor of Nihon-Ja
Ranger's Apprentice: The Kings of Clonmel
Ranger's Apprentice: The Lost Stories
The Ring of Solomon
The Scorpio Races
Starry River of the Sky
A Tale Dark and Grimm
Warriors: Omen of the Stars: Night Whispers
Warriors: Omen of the Stars: Sign of the Moon
Wonderstruck
A Wrinkle in Time: The Graphic Novel

Folklore
Cinder
Clare Beaton's Farmyard Rhymes
Clever Jack Takes the Cake
Hey Diddle Diddle and Other Favorite Nursery Rhymes
Jack and the Beanstalk
Monkey: A Trickster Tale from India
Muu, Moo! Rimas de animales / Animal Nursery Rhymes
The Neighborhood Sing-Along
*Nursery Rhyme Comics: 50 Timeless Rhymes from 50 Celebrated
    Cartoonists*
Puss in Boots
The Red Hen
A Tale Dark and Grimm
The Tooth Fairy Meets El Ratón Pérez
Trickster: Native American Tales: A Graphic Collection

Fractured Folk Tale
Animal Crackers Fly the Coop
The Cazuela That the Farm Maiden Stirred
Goldilocks and the Three Dinosaurs
The Little Red Pen
Three Little Pigs: An Architectural Tale

Friendship
Bink & Gollie
Liar & Spy
You Can Be a Friend

Historical Fiction
90 Miles to Havana
Between Shades of Gray
Breaking Stalin's Nose
Countdown
The Dreamer
The Extraordinary Mark Twain (According to Susy)
Heart of a Samurai
Hurricane Dancers: The First Caribbean Pirate Shipwreck
Moon Over Manifest
Nathan Hale's Hazardous Tales: Big Bad Ironclad!
Nathan Hale's Hazardous Tales: One Dead Spy
One Crazy Summer
Turtle in Paradise
Zora and Me

History
Around the World
Heart and Soul: The Story of America and African Americans
Saga of the Sioux: An Adaptation of Dee Brown's Bury My Heart at Wounded Knee
Sit-In: How Four Friends Stood Up by Sitting Down
Titanic: Voices from the Disaster
Underground

Horror
Anya's Ghost

Informational
All the Water in the World
Coral Reefs
Dark Emperor and Other Poems of the Night

Do You Know Which Ones Will Grow?
Eight Days Gone
Family Pack
Farm
How Did That Get in My Lunchbox? The Story of Food
How to Clean a Hippopotamus: A Look at Unusual Animal Partnerships
The Human Body
Swirl by Swirl: Spirals in Nature
Thunder Birds: Nature's Flying Predators

Math
How Many Jelly Beans? A Giant Book of Giant Numbers!
The Rabbit Problem
Ready, Set, 100th Day!

Music
Acoustic Rooster and His Barnyard Band
Squeak, Rumble, Whomp! Whomp! Whomp! A Sonic Adventure

Mystery
Anya's Ghost
The Candymakers
Fake Mustache: How Jodie O'Rodeo and Her Wonder Horse (and Some Nerdy Kid) Saved the U.S. Presidential Election from a Mad Genius Criminal Mastermind
Griffin & Co. Adventures: Framed
Griffin & Co. Adventures: Showoff
Guinea PIG, Pet Shop Private Eye: Fish You Were Here
Guinea PIG, Pet Shop Private Eye: The Ferret's a Foot
J. J. Tully Mystery: The Trouble with Chickens
Liar & Spy
Trash
Western Mysteries: The Case of the Deadly Desperados

Mythology
Olympians: Athena: Grey-Eyed Goddess
Olympians: Hades: Lord of the Dead

Olympians: Hera: The Goddess and Her Glory
Olympians: Zeus: King of the Gods
*Treasury of Greek Mythology: Classic Stories of Gods, Goddesses, Heroes
    & Monsters*

Nature
And Then It's Spring
Coral Reefs
Dark Emperor and Other Poems of the Night
Island: A Story of the Galápagos

Religion
All Things Bright and Beautiful
*Brother Sun, Sister Moon: Saint Francis of Assisi's Canticle of the
    Creatures*
Who Built the Stable? A Nativity Poem

Science Fiction
Bad Island
The Dead
Legend
Zig and Wikki in the Cow
Zita the Spacegirl: Legends of Zita the Spacegirl
Zita the Spacegirl: Zita the Spacegirl

Special Needs
Chunk Close: Face Book
My Brother Charlie
Out of My Mind
Wonder

Sports
The Batboy
Goal!
The Underdogs

Trains
Trains Go

Books for a Diverse Collection

90 Miles to Havana
Abraham Lincoln & Frederick Douglass: The Story behind an American Friendship
All the Way to America: The Story of a Big Italian Family and a Little Shovel
Annie and Helen
The Artist Who Painted a Blue Horse
Auntie Yang's Great Soybean Picnic
A Beach Tail
Big Red Lollipop
Big Wig: A Little History of Hair
The Cazuela That the Farm Maiden Stirred
Chavela and the Magic Bubble
Chickadee
The Christmas Coat
Dave the Potter: Artist, Poet, Slave
Dear Primo: A Letter to My Cousin
Diego Rivera: His World and Ours
Don't Call Me Hero
Drama
Drawing from Memory
The Dreamer
Dyamonde Daniel Books: Almost Zero
Dyamonde Daniel Books: Halfway to Perfect

Each Kindness
East Dragon, West Dragon
Eight Days: A Story of Haiti
Fiesta Babies
The Grand Plan to Fix Everything
Hand in Hand: Ten Black Men Who Changed America
Heart and Soul: The Story of America and African Americans
Heart of a Samurai
The House Baba Built: An Artist's Childhood in China
Hurricane Dancers: The First Caribbean Pirate Shipwreck
I, Too, Am America
I Have a Dream: Dr. Martin Luther King, Jr.
Inside Out and Back Again
It Jes' Happened: When Bill Traylor Started to Draw
Jimi: Sounds like a Rainbow
Ladder to the Moon
Liberty Porter, First Daughter: Cleared for Takeoff
Liberty Porter, First Daughter: Liberty Porter, First Daughter
Liberty Porter, First Daughter: New Girl in Town
Ling & Ting: Not Exactly the Same!
A Long Walk to Water: Based on a True Story
Lottie Paris Lives Here
Marisol McDonald Doesn't Match / Marisol McDonald no combina
*Maximilian & the Mystery of the Guardian Angel: A Bilingual Lucha
    Libre Thriller*
Me, Frida
The Mighty Miss Malone
Monkey: A Trickster Tale from India
Muu, Moo! Rimas de animales / Animal Nursery Rhymes
My Brother Charlie
A Nation's Hope
The Neighborhood Sing-Along
Ninth Ward
Of Thee I Sing: A Letter to My Daughters
One Crazy Summer
Out of My Mind
Pecan Pie Baby

Popularity Papers: Research for the Social Improvement and General Betterment of Lydia Goldblatt & Julie Graham-Chang

Popularity Papers: The Long-Distance Dispatch between Lydia Goldblatt & Julie Graham-Chang

Popularity Papers: The Rocky Road Trip of Lydia Goldblatt & Julie Graham-Chang

Popularity Papers: Words of (Questionable) Wisdom from Lydia Goldblatt & Julie Graham-Chang

Saga of the Sioux: An Adaptation of Dee Brown's Bury My Heart at Wounded Knee

Sit-In: How Four Friends Stood Up by Sitting Down

So For Real: Cool like That

Spike the Mixed-Up Monster

Squeak, Rumble, Whomp! Whomp! Whomp! A Sonic Adventure

Starry River of the Sky

Sugar Plum Ballerinas: Dancing Diva

Sugar Plum Ballerinas: Perfectly Prima

Sugar Plum Ballerinas: Sugar Plums to the Rescue!

Sugar Plum Ballerinas: Terrible Terrel

Summer Jackson: Grown Up

Tía Isa Wants a Car

The Tooth Fairy Meets El Ratón Pérez

Trickster: Native American Tales: A Graphic Collection

Underground

Walking on Earth and Touching the Sky: Poetry and Prose by Lakota Youth at Red Cloud Indian School

We Could Be Brothers

What's Special about Me, Mama?

Who Was Rosa Parks?

Wonder

The Wonder of Charlie Anne

You Can Be a Friend

Zora and Me

Author/Title Index